WORLD INSECURITY

INTERDEPENDENCE VULNERABILITIES, THREATS AND RISKS

PHILIPPE A. W. FRANZKOWIAK
MIGUEL C. VILOMBO
AIMAD EL OUARDANI

authorHOUSE®

AuthorHouse™ UK Ltd.
1663 Liberty Drive
Bloomington, IN 47403 USA
www.authorhouse.co.uk
Phone: 0800.197.4150

Published by AuthorHouse   03/26/2014

ISBN: 978-1-4918-9685-3 (sc)
ISBN: 978-1-4918-9686-0 (e)

Table of Contents

CHAPTER III

CHAPTER IV

ACKNOWLEDGEMENTS

We would like to thank Ms. Jessica Mathewson of the David Lubin (FAO) help desk for her generous support in providing us with journal articles pertinent to the subject we were investigating. We also would like to thank Mr. Malo Meshack, Adrian Cullis, Mr. Luigi Baldassari, and Mr. Remi Nono-Womdim-who linked us with a supportive network of experts and academics.

INTRODUCTION

The world is interdependent. It does not matter whether nations are big or small, weak or strong: this interdependence means, whenever a crisis, natural or manmade, emerges, all nations are potentially tangled up in crisis management. In the face of today's threats, vulnerabilities and risks are equally shared. Specifically, violence, conflict, political instability and statehood security governance are the drivers of food insecurity and famine in the world today: millions of people in countries and regions prone to instability and crises are experiencing food insecurity. To understand the concept of insecurity, it is necessary to take a look at its root causes, which can be divided into two categories: natural and structural. Structural root causes are often manmade and are not incidental in their nature and scope. As a result of human actions and decisions, countries with weak governments and governance structures are becoming more and more food insecure. Political instability, institutional crisis, constitutional order disruptions, weak statehood security and governance can generate, and even strengthen, further interconnected problems such as transnational organized crime, terrorism, religious extremism, as well as general socio-economic disorder, and recognizing this fact is of paramount importance.

In weak and fragile states, the lack of minimum governmental social safety nets has led to many thousands of otherwise preventable deaths in our post-Cold War world. These issues are global and affect Latin America, the Middle East, Asia and Africa. The security and stability of a State are mandatory requirements without which nothing can be achieved in other areas. Without security, there is no hope; without hope, there can be no commitment to a common future. There is a link between armed conflicts and food insecurity, which can eventually lead to confrontations between organs of the state. The state may opt to defend its interests and legitimacy, its national security and territorial integrity, without engaging in the process of addressing the root causes of violent conflict. In most cases, societal and institutional paralysis is the result of such conflict. The role of the institutions of governance is crucial in enabling the translation of policy into action. Armed conflicts have negative impacts at every level, from the community to the national and regional level. Since the end of the Cold War, the number of violent conflicts and political crises in Africa, Asia, Latin America and the Middle East has exploded. Some of these conflicts have become virtually chronic in their nature and scope. These unending conflicts have long-term consequences on societal progress and sustainable development due to the organic disruptions of the communities' foundations. In places affected by violent conflicts, self-sufficiency and agriculture have been hampered for decades. Rural areas, where the poorest often rely on small scale farming to survive, have become the theatre of massacres and general violence, resulting in a mass exodus from land, now considered too dangerous, that once provided a livelihood to entire communities. Chronic violent conflicts have also created a culture of dependency on humanitarian relief efforts. The trauma of being forced to live a nomadic life is dramatic in its psychological, sociological and anthropological effects, as people have to learn the art of coping with a life at the level of being vagabonds. The United Nations High Commission for Refugees (2013 report), estimated that about two-thirds of the world's population are forcibly uprooted people displaced within their own countries. Where there is a culture of chronic conflict political violence, hunger and malnutrition go hand in hand. In the most dramatic scenarios adversaries starve opponents into submission by seizing and destroying food stocks, by killing livestock and disrupting the food-production capacity, by cutting off food supplies and diverting food relief from intended beneficiaries to the military and their supporters, so as to maintain the status quo. In some cases, land mines are even placed in agricultural land in order to scare away the farmers and their families, who flee and seldom return, thus worsening the food production and economic development situation. It should be noted that the disruption of food production capacity in one area or country can also generate food deficits in other areas or countries, impacts are therefore never only local. The end of hostilities does not necessarily mean that food insecurity disappears: some regions have already experienced what is called post-emergency food shortages, as it sometimes takes a long time to return to a satisfactory level of food production, and the more an area has been affected by armed conflicts and violence, the longer it takes to tackle the hunger issue. *Protracted conflicts create an environment of constant refugee mobility: displaced people are trapped in a cycle of violence that causes hunger, denigration, hopelessness and perpetual terror.*

The impact of humanitarian and security problems often become a shared burden for the affected country and for the international community. As we have already mentioned, internal insecurity and instability usually emanate from the weakness of the institutions of governance, and this weakness can spread and affect a whole region. In the last few years, we have seen some examples that perfectly illustrate this situation. Post-Gaddafi Libya has been affected by internal chaos and violence, eventually contaminating neigbouring Mali, one of the first victims of a spillover from the unstable situation in Libyan. One of the consequences of these regional spillover effects is that they often lead to interventions led by international organizations to secure entire countries and to rebuild institutions of governance, but at a very high cost. When a country loses its control over part of its territorial jurisdiction, the "rogue" part of the country becomes a breeding ground for extremism, radicalism and terrorism. Such was the case of Mali, where France, backed by the UN, intervened to prevent its territorial disintegration as the Northern part of Mali wanted to secede. The latest crisis of Mali showed the world how political instability and social upheaval can lead to devastating consequences regarding a country's unity and historical values. Poor statehood governance can result in perpetuated fragility: the risk is that fragile states can be entangled into a dangerous cycle created by their own misfortune, a cycle that is aggravated by the lack of economic development. As a result of this, food insecurity turns into a long-term and chronic issue, slowly taking root in said country's society. In some cases, the combination of natural and structural causes can be devastating. Somalia has been suffering from chronic food insecurity since the 1990s due to the failure of its institutions of governance and made worse by chronic droughts, where one of the main consequence has been that millions of people in the Horn of Africa have been displaced to neighboring countries, in particular Kenya, Djibouti and Ethiopia. The effects of armed conflicts are particularly severe in Africa. The legacy of violent conflict includes the destruction of infrastructure, schools, health-care facilities and a drastic reduction in the governmental revenue base. For example, since March 2013 in Central African Republic, all schools in the country have been shut down due to the Sekela (Muslim) and Baleka (Christian) interreligious attacks and counter-attacks. This means that the future of the young generation has been put into jeopardy because of the current insecurity situation in the country. According to the World Bank, the legacies of conflicts place a heavy burden on post-conflict societies, making it difficult for them to rebuild successfully and to stabilize their societies. In many cases, the government has to restart from zero to re-establish itself by introducing a new governmental plan, which usually does not include any long term strategy to make food security accessible to everyone.

In recent years the interdependence of threats-vulnerabilities-and risks and their impacts were bought to global attention when acts of piracy threatened the safety of international maritime commerce. The constant hijacking of commercial vessels and individual persons, particularly off the coasts of Somalia and in the Gulf of Guinea is a clear indicator of the interdependence of threats and risks. Meanwhile, the most populated country of Africa, Nigeria has been struggling against Boko Haram, a terrorist organization. The consequences of both piracy and terrorism have been made worse by their links with transnational organized crime, thus contributing to their worldwide impacts for issues that were once only local or regional. As David Kaplan foresaw in 1994, the post-Cold War changes in world order has impacted West Africa in such a way that twenty years later, the region has become a threat to international peace and security.

In the years to come, conflicts could emerge over a new cause: water. Water is the most precious resource of this planet and its scarcity could eventually trigger armed conflicts between sovereign states in areas where water scarcity is increasing. Such conflicts are likely to happen in the next decades in regions such as the Middle East or East Africa. In order to prevent this, conflict management through international instruments and the implementation of regional and sub-regional trans-boundary management systems are of the utmost importance. They have already proven their efficiency in some cases: the Nile Basin Initiative, for example is trying to guarantee an equal share of the Nile waters between upstream and downstream countries; the bilateral treaties between Jordan and Israel are another proof that water, despite its scarcity and importance, can be shared in a peaceful way. However, the fact that many of the world's most arid places are also those where the population is increasing at a very fast rate can render the preventive resolution of conflicts through agreements over water sharing more difficult to achieve.

This book is divided into four sections: The first deals with the politics of food security. It deals with the concepts and definitions, including structural causes that trigger food insecurity globally. It includes an analysis of the decision-making process and the paralysis of sub-regional and regional institutions in times of crisis. It also has an analysis of statehood weakness, governance fragility, political crises and institutional paralysis in sub-regional, regional and international crisis management situations. The second deals with the understanding of the need for a security consensus where the importance of security involves every level. This chapter is about the importance of water as a national security asset and issue. It is an analysis of how trans-boundary water management systems initiatives at the regional and sub-regional levels and preventive conflict management mechanisms help prevent the outbreak of war, thanks to the use of international instruments, such as multilateral treaties and conventions. The third section looks at the practical nature of the contemporary world's interdependence and the vulnerabilities and risks involved, such as the impacts of organized crime, extremism and terrorism. It analyses how the Libyan aftermath is affecting the security stability of the Sahel region's neighbouring countries, and why Mali became the first victim of religious extremism, radicalism and terrorism. It also talks about the problem of piracy in the Gulf of Guinea, as well as a brief summary on the socioeconomic and political effects of extremism in Nigeria from Boko Haram, how it affects the stability in the Northern part of the country and also how this affects food security and agricultural sustainability there. The fourth section seeks to address the basic question about who pays the cost of armed conflicts, assesses the impacts and consequences on statehood security governance in terms of economic development strategies, and talks about the costs of armed conflicts both in terms of the financial and human resource commitments associated with chaotic states and their neighbours. We therefore conclude that in many parts of the world the security situation is deteriorating: it has become unpredictable and dangerous it is therefore of paramount importance to understand the best preventive strategies to employ before these manmade crises spiral completely out of control. The main risk is that post-conflict societies might just keep moving from one crisis to another: when peace agreements are broken the consequence is that any national strategic objectives are short lived, making developmental progress impossible.

P. Franzkowiak

M. Vilombo

A. El Ouardani

Rome, 20 March 2014

ACRONYMS

CBFP   Congo Basin Forest Partnership
DFAT   Australian Department of Foreign Affairs and Trade
DMU   Disaster Management Unit
ECOWAS   Economic Community of West African States
EDPRS   Economic Development and Poverty Reduction Strategy
EU   European Union
FAO   Food and Agriculture Organization
IMF   International Monetary Fund
MDG   Millennium Development Goal
NBI   Nile Basin Initiative
OECD   Organization for Economic Co-peration and Development
OPEC   Organization of Petroleum Exporting Countries
PCEA   Post-conflict environmental assessment
UN   United Nations
UNAIDS   Joint United Nations Programme on HIV/AIDS
UNCED   United Nations Conference on Environment and Development
UNCTAD   United Nations Conference on Trade and Development
UNDP   United Nations Development Programme
UNEP   United Nations Environment Programme
UNHCR   United Nations High Commissioner for Refugees
UNICEF   United Nations Children's Fund
UNRISD   United Nations Research Institute for Social Development
USAID   U.S Agency for International Development
WFP   World Food Programme
WHO   World Health Organization
WTO   World Trade Organization

CHAPTER I

The politics of food security

There are four basic principles that constitute food security: availability, access, utilization and stability. The nutritional dimension is integral to the concept of food security and to the work of those who try to improve it.[1] Food Security is therefore a human rights issue as, "the right of everyone to an adequate standard of living for himself and his family, including adequate food (. . .) and to the continuous improvement of living conditions as well as the fundamental right of everyone to be free from hunger"[2]. At the World Food Conference of 1974, food security was a matter of central importance: responsibility for food security was placed largely at the national level with an emphasis on the maintenance of a network of sufficient food reserves to meet the needs of a country. Food availability addresses the "supply side" of food security and is determined by the levels of food production, stock levels and net trade. An adequate supply of food at the national or international level does not in itself guarantee food security at the household level. Concerns about insufficient food access have resulted in a greater policy focus on incomes, expenditures, markets and prices in order to achieve food security objectives. The concept of *seasonal* food security falls between chronic and transitory food insecurity. It is similar to chronic food insecurity, as it is usually predictable and follows a sequence of known events. However, as seasonal food insecurity is of limited duration it can also be seen as recurrent, but transitory in nature. It occurs when there is a cyclical pattern of inadequate availability

---

[1]   Integrating food and nutrition security into country food analysis and UNDAF October 2011

[2]   States party to the International Covenant on Economic, Social and Cultural Rights (ICESCR)xvii of 1966, recognized:

and access to food. The dynamic nature of food security is implicit when we talk about people who could be vulnerable to food insecurity. While poverty encompasses different dimensions of deprivation that relate to human capabilities including consumption and food security, health, education, rights, having a voice, security, dignity and decent working conditions. Chronic hunger is a condition of life in which people are habitually undernourished, (Trueba and MacMillan, 2011:22). The 2002 World Food Summit Plan of Action opening statement reads: "Armed conflicts are enemies of food security. There is a well-established correlation between the exposure of countries to external or internal conflicts, and the deterioration or long-term stagnation in their food security. Most conflicts, and especially the internal conflicts that have now become the dominant model of mass violence, mainly affect rural areas and their populations. They disrupt food production through physical destruction and plundering of crops and livestock, harvests and food reserves; they prevent and discourage farming; they interrupt the lines of transportation through which food exchanges, and even humanitarian relief, take place; they destroy farm capital, conscript young and able-bodied males, taking them away from farm work and suppress income earning occupations. The impact of conflict on food security often lasts long after the violence has subsided, as assets have been destroyed, people killed or maimed, populations displaced, the environment damaged, and health, education and social services shattered; still more awesome are the landmines which litter the countryside.[3]" Conflicts bring about abrupt changes to both local and national governance. For example, a country might end-up having different local authorities where tax structure and the pace of development are different from the rest of the country, as is the case in Somalia, regarding Puntland and Somaliland. Each authority has its own government and the security forces are answerable to the regional leadership. The provision of basic goods and services through regular supply routes can be disrupted, and transportation becomes slow, risky, and expensive for poor people who depend on these services for their livelihood in order to survive. In Syria local populations face ever more acute food shortages and price rises as the spreading civil war makes agricultural production levels tumble and

---

[3]   World Food Summit10-13, 2002/ FAO-Rome.

threatens damage to staple crops, such as wheat and barley. Indeed political instability, armed conflicts and insecurity always emanate from unresolved interstate and intrastate quarrels. There are many examples around the world of high-profile unresolved quarrels, such as the Israeli and Palestinian issue in the Middle East, or the Kashmir border demarcation dispute between India and Pakistan. There are also unresolved issues in Somalia, in the Democratic Republic of Congo, in Nigeria where the government is fighting extremists, in Guinea Bissau, and in the Central African Republic. Sudan faces unresolved issues regarding the crisis in Darfur, as well as border and energy disputes with South Sudan, and Colombia has been fighting against the FARC rebels for decades. These redundant crises never cease regardless of political settlements, such as power-sharing structure deals, constitutional amendments and inclusions in the government. Rebellions led by senior officers who alleged that previously agreed upon commitments had not been fulfilled are very frequent, as was the case in the Democratic Republic of Congo. Religious extremism may stand against a new inclusive government, accusing its formation as being contrary to the public interest and therefore opting to fuel war in order to maintain the status quo, which guarantees them much broader benefits. Active armed conflicts contribute to hunger and chronic food insecurity, particularly if the conflict itself is used as a deliberate weapon to deny access to food for those in need of a basic subsistence, resulting in famine and death. This dramatic scenario occurs where adversaries starve opponents into submission by seizing, destroying food stocks, killing livestock, disrupting food-production capacity, cutting off food supplies and diverting food relief from intended beneficiaries to the military and their supporters. In countries affected by recurring armed conflicts, the chronic food insecurity strategy targets the rural community by uprooting them in order to force them to abandon their farming lands, thanks to direct attacks, terror, enslavement, or through the forced recruitment of its young people into militant ranks. As farming populations flee, decline, or stop farming out of fear, production falls—spreading food deficits over wider areas. During the conflicts in Angola, Mozambique and in Vietnam, there was a deliberate strategy to place land mines in cultivated fields, so as to hamper the production capacity of the agricultural system of these countries, which would result in food shortages in the longer-term. The land mines forced farmers to leave their fields, never to return, thus interrupting food production and economic activities. All these acts are linked to armed conflicts. Protracted conflicts create an environment of permanent refugee mobility. The refugees find themselves trapped in a cycle of violence that causes hunger, denigration, hopelessness and perpetual terror. Countries in the vicinity of failed and chaotic states are brought into a prisoner dilemma[4], having to decide whether to close their borders or to respect international commitments by providing humanitarian assistance to the refugees trapped in perpetual poverty. Despair emanates from political instability and statehood mismanagement of the institutions of governance. This situation eventually becomes a breeding ground for human rights violations resulting from current conflicts and rising violence. The costs are measured in deaths, broken lives, destroyed livelihoods, losses of homes, and increased vulnerability as those who are caught up in the cycle of armed violence become the by-product of the perpetrators who seek for national, regional and, to some extent, international legitimacy.

As violence increases the circle of vulnerability becomes a more important development issue. This is due to a number of factors including worldwide increases in everyday violence, the globalization of crime and violence, and the recognition that violence undermines economic growth and sustainable development (Mcllwaine, 1999:433). Structural economic vulnerability is one of the main problems faced by many developing countries that also face food security (Guillaumont, 2009:173). Legitimacy increases effectiveness

---

[4]   Definition from the Library of Economics and Liberty: *The prisoners' dilemma is the best-known game of strategy in social science. It helps us understand what governs the balance between cooperation and competition in business, in politics, and in social settings. In the traditional version of the game, the police have arrested two suspects and are interrogating them in separate rooms. Each can either confess, thereby implicating the other, or keep silent. No matter what the other suspect does, each can improve his own position by confessing. If the other confesses, then one had better do the same to avoid the especially harsh sentence that awaits a recalcitrant holdout. If the other keeps silent, then one can obtain the favorable treatment accorded a state's witness by confessing. Thus, confession is the dominant strategy (see game theory) for each. But when both confess, the outcome is worse for both than when both keep silent. The concept of the prisoners' dilemma was developed by RAND Corporation scientists Merrill Flood and Melvin Dresher and was formalized by Albert W. Tucker, a Princeton mathematician.* http://www.econlib.org/library/Enc/PrisonersDilemma.html

in governability of the state and territory. Good governance comprises the dimensions of legitimacy and effectiveness to facilitate governability with the consent of the society. Without legitimacy the government finds it increasingly difficult to govern without reverting to coercive and oppressive means, and risks getting involved in a downward-spiralling process—losing control and legitimacy at the same time (Berendsen and Beuningen 2008:73). Democratic societies have what experts call 'open government', that displays three main characteristics: transparency—its actions, and the individuals responsible for those actions, will be exposed to public scrutiny and challenge; accessibility—its services and information on its activities will be readily accessible to citizens; responsiveness—it will be responsive to new ideas, demands and needs. Democracy enables legitimacy and effectiveness, governance and governability. Democracy consists of smooth relations in the exercise of power on one hand and, on the other hand, of mechanisms to control, limit, and disperse power through a system of checks and balances.

The causes of economic stagnation are both structural and non-structural variables, for example geography and governance. Countries at war maintain one of the last bastions of famine in the contemporary world. Almost every famine in the last 30 years has been connected with armed conflicts of one sort or another. The connection is particularly evident in Sub-Saharan Africa, where conflict-related famines have struck country after country—Angola, Ethiopia, Kenya, Mozambique, Nigeria, Somalia, Sudan, Uganda, to name a few. The two main food crises of the 1990s outside Africa, in Iraq and North Korea, were also related to military hostilities. In countries where a number of people live in extreme poverty, the political leadership somehow shares the burden due to the lack of basic social safety nets. The lack of adequate political and strategic leadership contributes to the famine outbreak. Democratic societies often respond adequately to famine and create safety nets for food resilience because these safety nets are embodied in the democratic tissues and are part of the social contract between the people and its government. The following factors trigger famine: recession, aggregate output and income decline, and the physical disruption of agricultural production. The war economies sometimes do quite well in terms of aggregate output. However, the shifting of production to supply the military forces leads to severe shortages for civilians and trigger sharp price increases for essential commodities, such as wheat and maize, while an increased effort is dedicated to the development and the upkeep of the industries that are necessary to fight the war. This happens especially in Africa's poorest countries that are involved in both intra and inter-state conflicts and use the available resources for the defence of their so-called national security and sovereignty. This means that in the name of national security and national sovereignty, the government's priority is to invest in military hardware infrastructure. The debt of most poor nations has been accumulated as a consequence of bilateral state-to-state business to obtain military hardware. Such was the case of Angola: during the war much of the attention was focused on sustaining national security and sovereignty, all of which made the acquiring of defence equipments and other related assets and infrastructures become the priority of the government of Angola, remaining at the top of the country's decision making list from 1975 to 2002.

Many areas of Africa have experienced more violent armed conflicts than any other continent in recent decades, with civil wars, localized violence, and a general lack of security plaguing many countries. The toll on human lives has been enormous; armed conflicts cause as many deaths as epidemics in Africa each year and they are responsible for more deaths and displacement than famine or floods. Between 1998 and 2002, some four million people died in in the Democratic Republic of Congo civil war alone. When people are forced to flee their homes, malnutrition and disease inevitably follow. Those who suffer the most from violence are people who are poor and vulnerable, including women and children. There are 13 million internally displaced people in Africa, mostly as a result of violent conflicts, and 3.5 million refugees. The situation remains serious. Without security, and without greater and more successful efforts aimed at preventing violent conflicts, Africa will not achieve its economic or human development goals. The causes of conflict are complex: exclusion, poor political and economic governance, judicial failure, dependency and natural resources[5]. Agricultural activities can be disrupted either for a

---

[5]   Report of the Commission for Africa 2005:105-7.

short or long period of time. Poverty, economic inequality and lack of development are complex in their nature and scope as they have multiple causes and therefore require multiple remedies to address them. According to Professor Amartya Sen, the conceptualization and measurement of poverty has two requirements, identified as: (1) a method of identifying a group of people as poor (identification), and (2) a method of aggregating the characteristics of the set of poor people into an overall image of poverty (aggregation). As a foundation for these, a study should take an inventory of the approaches that can be used. These include the biological (minimum nutritional requirement) and inequality approaches to poverty, the concept of relative deprivation, value judgement, policy definition, common standards for comparisons between communities, and the relative scaling of deprivation as a means of aggregation[6]. The Asia and Pacific region countries are making outstanding progress in the race towards achieving the 2015 Millennium Development Goals, regarding the reduction of poverty and food insecurity in China and South East Asia[7].

Let's work together

The fight against poverty, food insecurity and malnutrition requires a constructive engagement through a spirit of dialogue with member countries and other positive actors.

The FAO has set strategies for working with civil society and the private sector[8]. The United Nations System leadership emphasises the importance of civil society involvement in addressing peace and security, food security, and sustainable economic development. This engagement requires undivided attention from proactive actors at all levels: community, national, sub-regional—regional and global levels. This means that all stakeholders must make efforts together towards greater achievement,

---

[6]   Amartya Sen (1982), *Poverty and Famines: An Essay on Entitlement and Deprivation*, Oxford University Press

[7]   UNESCAP-Mr. Raj Kumar-Poverty and Development Division-Millennium— Development Goals-in the Region.

[8]   The new FAO and Civil Society Strategic partnership, approved at the 145 Council Strategy April 2013,

as it is summed up in the following quote: "it is possible to end hunger if we work together"[9]. The civil society, or societies, is defined as: "social movements who organize themselves around objectives, constituencies, and thematic interests"[10]. Civil society is a broad category which encompasses a wide variety of organizations, which although different, often share certain common goals, resources and/or approaches to maximize their decision-making capacity[11]. The need for cooperation has never been as great as in the current world, with its constantly shifting challenges.

The United Nations system is best placed to provide a platform for coordinated international action by virtue of its good standing and legitimacy. It is also strengthened by a universal membership allowing for consensus to adopt inclusive decision-making processes as tools for international peace, security, stability and prosperity[12]. There is a common concern among all stakeholders engaged in the fight against poverty and food insecurity, as Mr. Yaya Olaniran commented: "poverty and hunger is the common enemy, Africans should produce more food to enable food sovereignty in the region[13]." This cannot be achieved alone and without cooperation. According to the Report, "The State of Food Insecurity in the World 2012" published by FAO there are both good and bad news. The bad news is that in Africa, in particular Sub-Saharan Africa, food insecurity is still high compared to Asia and Latin America. However despite the negative news ranking Sub-Saharan Africa as the most food-insecure

---

[9] FAO Chief Jose Graziano Da Silva closing Statement to FAO Council on *26, April 2013*

[10] United Nations General Assembly A/53/170 "Arrangements and practices for the interaction of non-governmental organizations in all activities of the United Nations System" A/53/170: July 10, 1998.

[11] United Nations organizes and hosts, on a regular basis, briefings, meetings and conferences for NGOs representatives who are accredited to United Nations offices, programmes and agencies.

[12] United Nations and Civil Society, Economic and Social Council resolution 1297 (XLIV http://www.un.org/en/civilsociety/

[13] Mr Yaya Olaniran, Chair of the Committee on Food Security (CFS), FAO Regional Conference for Africa Brazzaville, 23-27 April 2012

region, there is a positive aspect since there are today fewer hungry people in the world than 20 years ago. This statistic also includes Africa, and the progress made there is due to a series of measures. South-South cooperation has been on the rise every year but above all this, there is a fierce activism shown by the emerging economies of the South, who are stepping forward to provide technical and financial support to countries lagging behind in terms of human resources and knowledge. Since 1996, when the South-South Cooperation initiative was established, over fifty South-South Cooperation agreements have been signed and more than 1,600 developing country experts and technicians have been deployed to support other countries' agricultural development and food security initiatives[14]. The other good news is the rise of cooperation among positive actors. This was noted during the Addis Ababa meeting where African leaders, together with representatives of international organizations, civil society, the private sector, cooperatives, farmers, youth groups, academia and other partners, unanimously adopted a declaration aimed at ending hunger in Africa by 2025. FAO Director General Graziano da Silva commented: "international cooperation plays an important role in achieving the sustainable and hunger-free future we all want because, in the globalized world we live in today, it is impossible to achieve the eradication of hunger and extreme poverty without working together[15]". Food security requires a strong political commitment to let member states harmonize their national food security strategic policies, a point which is critical to foster economic growth, employment and the income earning capacities of the poorest, thereby increasing their access to food through sustainable agricultural development programmes. Before becoming the Director General of FAO, in his address to the member states, candidate Jose Graziano Da Silva articulated his election manifesto to the Council on how FAO, under his leadership, intended to eradicate hunger and successfully complete the agreed-upon reforms of FAO adding that the pertinent issues to tackle were the strengthening of South-to-South Cooperation, ending his presentation by saying: "*I will not be able to do anything except what we can*

---

[14]   The June 29th 2013, High Level Meeting of African and International Leaders

[15]   Lula da Silva, Kufuor: Political Commitment crucial to end hunger and food insecurity in Africa.

do together[16]. One year later, after assuming the leadership of FAO his vision of cooperation is slowly being implemented and is already showing efficiency, as shown in the following diagram.

The four elements of the diagram represent the following: multilateral technical assistance from the UN/FAO; sub-regional, regional policy and technical support platform; national government food security strategy; civil society and private business partnerships. All those are being transformed into tangible actions oriented towards a great degree of efficiency and effectiveness.

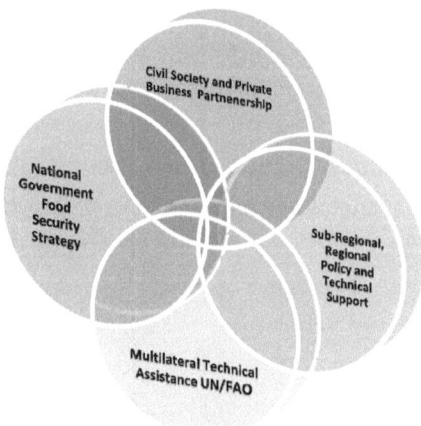

Today, the governments of the developing countries are becoming positive activists working towards Millennium Development Goals, especially in Asia, Africa and Latin America.

The idea that few countries from Sub-Sahara African nations would be able to set up a trust fund dedicated to agricultural development is an indicator of how peace and security are linked to economic development. On **June 16th 2013 in Rome**, FAO Director-General José Graziano Da Silva formally recognized 38 countries for having reduced hunger by half, well ahead of international targets set for the year 2015.

---

[16]   FAO-Council-Hundred and Forty, Rome, 28 November-2 December 2011.

During a high-level ceremony attended by several heads of state, 18 countries received diplomas for their early achievement of the targets set by the Millennium Development Goal 1 (MDG1) to halve the proportion of hungry people by 2015. Those 18 countries were also rewarded for their achievement of the more stringent World Food Summit (WFS) goals of halving the absolute number of hungry people by 2015. Those countries are: Armenia, Azerbaijan, Cuba, Djibouti, Georgia, Ghana, Guyana, Kuwait, Kyrgyzstan, Nicaragua, Peru, Saint Vincent and the Grenadines, Samoa, Sao Tome and Principe, Thailand, Turkmenistan, Venezuela and Viet Nam. A further twenty countries received diplomas for meeting the MDG 1-related target to halve hunger. They are: Algeria, Angola, Bangladesh, Benin, Brazil, Cambodia, Cameroon, Chile, Dominican Republic, Fiji, Honduras, Indonesia, Jordan, Malawi, Maldives, Niger, Nigeria, Panama, Togo and Uruguay. Recognition in both cases was based on hunger reductions achieved between 1990-92 and 2010-2012. The WFS goal was set in 1996, when 180 nations met at FAO headquarters to discuss ways to end hunger and the MDG 1 target was established by the international community at the United Nations General Assembly in 2000. On February 22nd 2013, Equatorial Guinea announced that it was making the first contribution, amounting to $30 million, for the "Africa for Africa" anti-hunger pool. The Africa Solidarity Trust Fund was made official in a ceremony at the margins of the third Africa-South America Summit[17] in Malabo, which was attended by FAO Director-General José Graziano Da Silva. Meeting with the President of Equatorial Guinea, Teodoro Obiang Nguema Mbasogo, before the signature of the donation agreement, Graziano da Silva said that the contribution was a sign of the country's commitment to the eradication of hunger in Africa. During FAO's April 2012 regional conference which was held in the Republic of Congo, President Denis Sassou Nguesso called for greater

---

[17] Africa-South America Summit (ASA) holds from 20-23 February 2013 in Malabo, Republic of Equatorial Guinea on the theme: "Strategies and Mechanisms to strengthen South-South Cooperation" to promote solidarity and partnership between South American and Africa, especially as they both share a common history and cultural.

solidarity between African nations to fight hunger.[18] **On June 20th 2013 in Rome,** Angola announced that it would give $10 million to the new Africa Solidarity Trust Fund administered by FAO, to be invested in promoting food security in Africa. This announcement was made by Afonso Pedro Canga, Minister of Agriculture and Rural Development of Angola during the 38th FAO Conference, the organization's highest governing body. Angola is one of the few post-conflict African countries that emerged from a multifaceted and multi-dimensional complex humanitarian emergency towards post-conflict developmental process phase with outstanding success. This success was made possible due to the peace and security that the country is enjoying since the end of the war, but also by the petro-dollars from its oil industry revenue. The success of the agricultural system requires a reliable access to financing, as well as high-quality seeds, fertilizers, and most importantly to a secured water system to enable adequate irrigation. Other essentials include access to robust markets that could absorb the higher level of agricultural output, a solid post-harvest value chain for the output of farmers, and programmes to train them in better practices so that they can improve their productivity. Africa has very varied agro-ecological conditions, so countries need to adopt many different farming models to create an African green revolution[19]. Many conflicts in the past prevented the local people from producing or accessing the means of production, due to the prevalent insecurity. In the absence of a local ability to produce food, conflicts often degenerate into a food crisis. The impacts of chronic conflicts are unpredictable and often hamper food production capacity because of the presence of constant security issues that threaten farmers at the local and national levels. Conventional wisdom teaches that chronic insecurity and political instability have long term consequences on human development, causing constant uncertainties that create an inadequate environment in which vulnerable people have to live. One dramatic consequence of this is that they become dependent on

---

[18]   African trust fund for food security becomes reality/ "Africa for Africa" anti-hunger pool;http://www.fao.org/news/story/pt/item/170278/icode/

[19]   The African Green Revolution Forum brings together many of the public and private organizations now investing in Africa's agricultural future of Africa's smallholder farmers. http:/ www.agrforum.com//

humanitarian aid for their livelihood. The longer a conflict lasts, the quicker the suffering people may seek the benefits provided by humanitarian aid, because their own country has or had poor food security resilience. Chronic food insecurity therefore depends on structural causes, as prolonged armed conflicts and political violence are undoubtedly the drivers of long term hunger and malnutrition. Conflicts, whether they are intra or inter-states, have negative consequences, and the resulting political instability destroys the institutions of governance which in turn hampers sustainable economic development.

Causal links

There are five causal links as seen in the diagram below: chronic conflicts, impacts, consequences, weak institutions of governance and food security safety nets. Indeed food insecurity, political instability and upheavals are some of the challenges facing national governments. The following graph shows how one wrong link or misstep leads to another and how armed conflicts and political crises lead to complex and multifaceted multidimensional humanitarian emergency situations and post-conflict emergency recovery crises. Chronic humanitarian and emergency led crises require a strong political will to resolve them. If there are weak institutions of governance, quarrels always appear as well as legitimacy issues. At the center of gravity is the struggle to seize power, and this is what drives the long unresolved crises in the Central African Republic and in the Democratic Republic of Congo. Rebellions often reappear and as a consequence millions are left without shelter and permanent settlement. This results in long term dependency on humanitarian relief emergency efforts. The immediate impacts are as follows: increased level of food insecurity and livelihood; increased number of displaced persons and refugees moving from one area to another. This is happening in certain parts of Africa, Asia and the Middle East. Food insecurity in the Sahel region is a perfect example of this, showing how food availability has been influenced by the weakness of states that have been facing conflicts, political unrest and instability for long periods of time, pulling them into a "chronic hunger crisis".

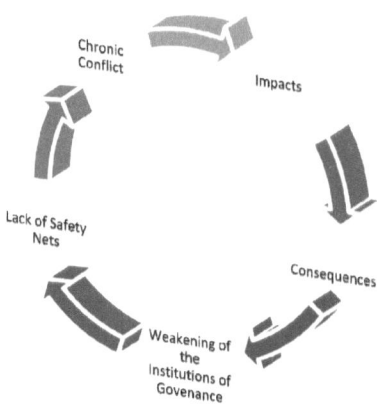

The root causes of political vulnerability emanate from power and legitimacy. Post-conflict societies suffer from this syndrome where power is concentrated in the hands of elites whose policies display little regard to the wider needs and concerns of the society. Ordinary citizens typically have no control over the state, and the state itself is usually limited in its ability to act through policy. The presence of a weak government incapable of enforcing the rule of law and easily co-opted by wealthy and powerful forces creates a difficult environment for progressive-minded individuals, forcing them to make uncomfortable choices. The impacts of weak statehood governance are many, according to Charles King (1997), and the structure of internal conflicts also contributes substantially to their duration. Structural variables include: faction leaders' personal commitments to the struggle; the difficulty of assessing the true battlefield situation and whether victory really is unattainable and the relatively weak command and control structures of many belligerent groups.

The Democratic Republic of Congo is a huge and complex country. The United Nations had been stuck there for years to mitigate the consequences of decades of political decay, economic stagnation and institutional crises. There are a number of countries in Sub-Saharan African where the major causes of insecurity are related to the way national organs of the state themselves manage security. This is a consequence of the combination of the fear of a lack of legitimacy and of the sudden loss of power. When the leadership is fearful of losing power due to a lack of legitimacy, the securitization of the state through a tunnel-vision strategy becomes part of its strategy and limits the leadership. A tunnel-vision strategy tends to overlook anything that is not representing the groupthink of the leadership inner-circle, only addressing security through one-way methods and neglecting other views. The problem associated with power centered leadership is that security governance becomes strictly exclusive, losing touch with reality on the ground-level where the real threats are biologically bred, gradually spreading like cancer within the entire country's societal tissue. As a consequence of this, the state fails. As Robert Bates put it, "many organized to suppress internal opposition rather than to defend against external threats". The conceptualization of "Failed States" is necessary to understand why their highly securitized construction represents a shift in assessing and understanding transnational security threats. Rotberg states that, "Nation-states fail when they are consumed by internal violence and cease delivering positive political goods to their inhabitants. Their governments lose credibility, and the continuing nature of the particular nation-state itself becomes questionable and illegitimate in the hearts and minds of its citizens. The concept describes the need to deliver positive political goods for the public. In other words, political goods are associated with a high level political strategic decision-making processes, and their successful delivery has to come through accountable institutions" (Rotberg, 2004:1-9).

This concept was used mainly to describe the shifting reality in International Relations where waves of non-state actors contributed greatly to the understanding of the 'failed state' concept. The concept does not contain any analytical aspect; however its elementary description highlights a solid basis for the comprehensive understanding of the dynamics associated with statehood failure. For example, states that have refugee camps for Internally Displaced People (IDPs) in which sometimes a generation was born and raised are more likely to be subject to failure. Without alternatives, those who are born in the camps are more likely to contribute to the expansion of insecurity, which in the end might delegitimize the central government. The variety of indicators to identify a weak, failing, failed or collapsed state illustrates the depth of the challenge of defining state failure. Nation-states are the normative framework in international relations; they are the embodiment of the political reality that governs people, guarantees law and security. A "Failed State", then, is still a member of the international system but its political reality is strikingly different: there is a huge gap between conceptual reality and practical reality. State security governance is very complicated in states that have poor economies, lack of or deteriorating civil society, and weak government institutions exploited by the elites. Failed state performance should be based on deliverance of political goods but instead is parasitized by elites that maintain a status quo, to the detriment of those in need. Regional, sub-regional and intra-state conflicts can spill over and affect other states. In fragile regions, conflicts may trigger exoduses and immigration, with people seeking protection from neighbouring countries. Accepting refugees is an international moral obligation for every state. The influx of refugees can have several repercussions. They may illegally occupy private or government lands; tensions might escalate near borders as refugees may bring their cattle with them, as is already the case in the Horn of Africa, and that may contribute to the destruction of forests and pastures; the refugees may use available resources such as firewood, water, and produce waste, putting additional strain and threatening the ecosystems in particular in areas where the exodus does not seem to stop because of prolonged conflicts (Michael Brown et al, 2004:324). Fragile states are widely recognized as a danger both to international security and to the security of their neighbors as well as to the well-being of their own people. Their lawless environments spread instability across borders and provide safe havens for terrorists, drug dealers, and weapons smugglers, endangering the access to natural resources and consigning millions to poverty. Fragile states are the source of much of the violence and many of the humanitarian crises around the world. Their societies thus become breeding grounds for criminals and extremists who disrupt the international order (Kaplan, 2008:2). Inadequate governance structures cannot ensure institutional stability, and the lack of transparency, accountability, an imbalanced rule of law that is discriminating against regionalist and ethnic groups, tribes, and economic exclusion lead to inefficient decisions that do more harm than good. The legacy of the conflicts in Sub-Saharan Africa has generational consequences. Armed conflicts have been the drivers of extreme impoverishment and food insecurity on the continent. Countries that lag behind in terms of economic development have had a long history of armed conflicts. The costs of conflicts are high in terms of slow economic progress, and thereby hamper positive initiatives aimed at alleviating poverty and economic development. Political leadership at the highest level is now generally marked by pragmatism when it comes to the monitoring of success and failure and by the implementation of a mechanism of accountability. The post-conflict developmental phase is the stage where overall a country's developmental strategic road maps are crafted, setting into motion the economic recovery based on a strong and accountable political leadership supported by partners located at all levels: local, national, sub-regional, regional and international. This process requires that an effective agent at the top to provide a provisional framework within which a structure of institutions can gradually be erected to allow the state to return to the centre of social and political organization in civil society. Legitimacy must be restored early on, through constructive participation and freely expressed support from society. It is necessary to provide a large, informally representative forum, and if the contenders for power do not do so, an external force to guarantee security and free expression during the legitimization process may be required. Resources need to be made available for reconstruction. It is hard to overcome the problems of neglect and misallocation that lay at the root of the state's collapse without some resources for the new state to manage. Foreign intervention may be needed to perform the functions of the collapsed state, but only until local forces can take over the business of putting the state back together. Preventive diplomacy is thus here defined as follows: action taken in vulnerable places and times to avoid the threat or use of armed force and related forms of coercion by states or groups to settle the political disputes that can arise from the destabilizing effects of economic, social, political, and international change. Crisis diplomacy or crisis management as it is more commonly called, conceptually lies on the opposite side of preventive diplomacy and involves efforts to manage tensions and disputes that are so intense that they have reached the level of confrontation. The threat of force by one or more party is common, and the actual outbreak of hostilities is highly likely (Michael Lund, 1996:292).

Kenya experienced political and humanitarian crises following the contested presidential election held on 27 December 2007. The Kenyan people were surprised, given the historical context and the particular moment in which the elections were held, in a country which for decades had enjoyed long-lasting peace and power successions without disruption. The world was surprised as they placed undivided trust upon the wisdom and judgment of the political leaders of Kenya to exercise constraints and care given the sensitive nature of the tourism industry, which depends on security, peace and stability. In 1989, the World Bank study on Africa's long-term perspectives concluded that the single most important challenge confronting African countries was the issues of statehood governance[20]. When looking for examples of strong institutions, Nordic and Scandinavian governments are often mentioned because of the quality of their bureaucratic systems and of the public services they provide to their people. Well-governed or strong states normally have the capacity to incontestably control the territories on which they have full jurisdiction. The rule of law prevails and the judiciary system is independent and separated from the executive power, two things that are necessary for good governance. In comparison, weak states do not provide such levels of political will. Weak states are constantly entangled in political and institutional crises. They can be weak because of their geographical location and economic constraints. The states can be weak because of internal antagonisms, management flaws of its political leadership, greed, or despotism. Weak states create an environment where religious fundamentalists and fanatics thrive, where tensions between communities that are sometimes centuries-old become overtly violent, and where the democratic political process is often stopped by disruptions of constitutional order. Weak states may have governments that target their own citizens, encourage or even cause armed conflicts, thus contributing to the escalation of criminal violence within state borders. State legitimacy is lost as the infrastructures deteriorate or are completely destroyed. The economy falters, and then collapses. The anarchic nature of some weak states, such as Somalia, the Democratic Republic of Congo, Guinea Bissau and Mali dragged them into political and economic crises. The collapse of the state infrastructure and societal failure are viewed on a continuum that are interconnected and interrelated to one another (Zartman 2005:7). Weak statehood institutions of governance often exhibit a vacuum of

---

[20]   World Bank, Sub-Saharan Africa: From Crisis to Sustainable Growth, A Long Term Perspective Study-Washington D.C (1989:60)

authority, a black hole into which a failed state has fallen. There is a dark energy, but the forces of entropy have overwhelmed the radiance that hitherto provided some order that is vital to common political goods to the citizens within the borders (Jackson, 1996:10-11). State collapse is both the cause and the result of internal or civil wars, as weak and illegitimate order permits violence and violence consumes legitimacy and order. Although no two cases of state collapse are the same and "collapse" can take on a variety of specific manifestations, the fundamental fact of the disappearance of state institutions, law, and order creates inhumanities and insecurities that affect the surrounding countries. The cumulative effects of poverty, overpopulation, rural flight and rapid urbanization, as well as environmental degradation, overwhelm the weak state to the point of collapse[21].

Dividend of peace

Why do peace, security and development matter? Peace and security are of paramount importance to the success of poverty reduction and are inseparable ingredients that lead to good statehood governance. Good governance is the driving force of economic and human empowerment. Sustainable development requires the support of a forward-looking leadership to shape the destiny of their countries. In Sub-Saharan Africa, some states are stuck in a post-conflict situation or are affected by recurring conflicts. The long term collateral damage that results from this evidently provokes more poverty and food insecurity, sometimes for decades. According to the World Bank, in order to facilitate transition towards sustainable peace after a prolonged period of hostilities, there needs to be a strong focus on economic and social development, especially by rebuilding the domestic markets and restoring the access to external resources such as technical and financial assistance. Post-conflict societies reconstruction assistance packages can jump-start the economy through investment in strategic sectors. These assistance packages are accompanied by foreign investment and promote macroeconomic stabilization as well as the rehabilitation of financial institutions. Re-establishing the frameworks

---

[21]   David Carment Third World Quarterly Vol. 24, No. 3, p. 414.

of regulation and governance by strengthening government institutions allows the civil society to work effectively. Meanwhile, targeting assistance to those affected by war is a must. This can be done through the repatriation of displaced populations, the demobilization of ex-combatants, by revitalizing the local communities that were among the most disrupted and supporting small scale agricultural development. Furthermore, it can be done by supporting landmine clearing action programs where relevant, as part of a comprehensive development strategy for areas populated with land mines. In doing so, a particular focus has to be adopted regarding vulnerable groups, such as households with female heads (World Bank, 1998:3). A number of Sub-Saharan, Asian, and Latin American countries received recognition for their effort to meet Millennium Development Goals targets. Among these countries, some have been involved in long conflicts. After a period of peace, political stability and good governance, these countries are gradually emerging from total dependency on food emergency aid. Instead, they are leaning towards a local strategic plan aimed at the improvement of food reliance. The plans are usually based on mechanisms dedicated to the stimulation of the agricultural sector in order to achieve long term resilience.

The progressive arrow in the next graph shows that post-conflict societies always depart from a disadvantageous place simply because the contradictions that led them into violent conflict have their own origins, which need to be addressed. The arrow shows what progress is needed for food security and economic development to happen in post-conflict societies: peace, security, and good statehood governance are fundamental in this process.

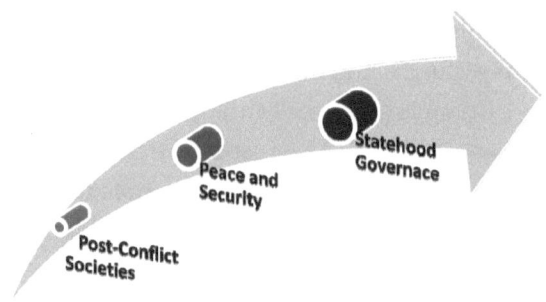

A post-conflict society requires peace and security, since without it no major economic development can be achieved. In post-conflict societies, governance is always scrutinized by various actors, both international and local, who are constantly questioning every action and decision. The actors who perform this task have high expectations and each of them do for their own reasons. Furthermore, accountability and transparency are entirely part of the process. A number of countries have emerged from their post-conflict society status to become successful economies through a responsible democratization process. It is obvious that when a war ends, the governments of the belligerent countries swiftly shift their national strategic agendas and priorities from national security towards the rehabilitation of social infrastructures and towards reconstruction and development. Countries that have successfully achieved outstanding results regarding this are those who have rehabilitated roads, railway-lines and power supply networks so as to enable economic development, with a focus on agricultural development. This was the case in Angola for example, after the end of a deadly conflict that lasted for decades. The government concentrated on rebuilding an efficient and competitive agricultural sector, which employs the majority of Angolan people in the rural areas for their livelihood. David White, of the Financial Times, recently called it "one of the fastest-growing places on Earth[22]. Angola however is not the only country that emerged from a post-conflict crisis to become one of the fastest growing economies on the continent. In Sub-Saharan Africa, there are other countries that have successfully changed their focus to rise from uncertainty and set sail towards economic emergence, success and development. Mozambique is one of them, and it is making remarkable progress in terms of economic development, attracting direct foreign investment aimed at the exploration of its natural resources, a potential huge source of wealth that could benefit the common good. The government of Mozambique put in place a positive, realistic and implementable contingent plan to alleviate food insecurity with both short term and long term related responses. Another country that emerged from a disastrous post-conflict crisis is Rwanda, a country that had to recover from a genocide in the mid-1990s. This country has achieved something unexpected, quickly restarting economic

---

[22]   The Financial Times, July 18th 2012.

development, achieving sustainable resilience, peace and securing its territory. Conventional wisdom suggests that Rwanda is the Israel of the Great Lakes Region, because it is one of the few well-governed, focused and disciplined countries in Sub-Saharan Africa. Leadership matters when it comes to strategic direction and focus and countries that are growing at an accelerated speed have one thing in common: they have learned that war had huge costs to their respective societal tissue. The concept of good governance has been adapted to further the World Bank's activities, and has been redefined in terms of effectiveness. As a shifting in reality happened in the post-cold war world, the conceptual understanding of "good governance" changed. It has become a precondition for sustainable development which entails among others things accountability in statehood governance. All subsidiaries from the international financial institutions or 'the World Group', such as the International Monetary Fund (IMF), include in their negotiations some good governance-related clauses. Globally there is a general consensus among policymakers, practitioners, academia, state and non-state actors that good governance is at the centre of gravity for economic growth, poverty reduction and food security. The good governance concept has a number of pieces in its mosaic. There are seven principles of good statehood governance. These are:

- *Participation:* entails that men and women should participate equally in the decision-making process, directly or indirectly, through legitimate intermediary institutions that represent their intentions, rights and expressions.

- *Consensus orientation:* good governance takes the interests of stakeholders into account, in an effort to reach a broad consensus even when it comes to policy issues, for the best interest of all.

- *Strategic vision:* it is a key to good statehood governance, necessary for long-term perspectives and human development. It is also useful in terms of soft power and leadership influence.

- *Responsiveness:* institutions and processes try to serve all stakeholders, and must therefore be highly effective and efficient, embracing a results-driven policy, maximizing savings and cost efficiency.

- *Accountability,* a system of accountability for decision-makers in a government is necessary, as well as in the private sector and civil society organizations, so that they can be held accountable for their action to the public, as well as to institutional stakeholders.

- *Transparency:* a transparency system with access to a free flow of public information, institutions and information. It has to be available to those concerned with such information, and to be provided with enough material to understand and monitor it.

- *Equity and Rule of Law:* all men and women are to enjoy a fair and impartial hearing from a competent court of law[23]. Equality before the law is aimed at strengthening democratic governance and the rule of law.

The former United Nations Secretary General Kofi Annan asserted that: "good governance and sustainable development are indivisible. That is the lesson of all our efforts and experiences, from Africa to Asia to Latin America. Without good governance—without the rule of law, predictable administration, legitimate power, and responsive regulation—no amount of funding, no amount of charity will set us on the path to prosperity." Security governance is therefore linked to the statehood capacity embodied in its institutions to ensure that national security and territorial integrity are adequately protected, that law enforcement agencies are well funded, that its security resources are of good quality, and that its personnel are skilled and trained to face the modern challenges, which are complex and multi-faceted in their nature and scope. The concept of governance in this context is applied to different situations, at different levels. In this context good statehood governance depends on the quality of the public services. It is vital to refocus the attention on the role public services play: when bureaucratic infrastructures are consolidated, reliable and competent, they

---

[23] UNDP Principles text on which they are based United Nations Universal Declaration of Human Rights Participation (Article 19)

are successful in delivering common goods and services. Strong institutions of good governance are self-regulated and interdependent, and thus make stability possible by guaranteeing a calm and fluid transition of power from one state leader to another.

According to US President Barack Obama, the four pillars of the "United States Strategy Towards Sub-Saharan Africa" are: the strengthening of democratic institutions; the stimulation of economic growth, trade, and investment; the advancement of peace and security; and the promotion of opportunity and development[24]. There are benefits associated with the application of the good governance principles in every institutional role dealing mutual benefits for the parties involved. The obvious one is the enabling environment of confidence that can attract top foreign investors who bring in new technologies, human and financial capital to turn natural resources into tangible wealth, thus creating new jobs and generating permanent income to the local people. The second benefit is the tax revenue for the national governments: the more revenue it has at its disposal, the more it can reinvest in critical strategic infrastructures. Mozambique in 1980s early 1990s was entangled in intra-state conflicts causing severe damage to its economy and to the societal tissue as a whole. Shortly after peace and security returned, the democratization process had created institutions of governance based on the rule of law, transparency and accountability, allowing investors to feel safe enough to invest. As a consequence many foreign companies have invested in Mozambique's oil and gas sectors since the conclusion of a prolonged civil war that ended in 1992. The World Bank classified Mozambique's transition from a post-conflict country to one of Africa's "frontier economies" and this turned it into a model for many countries in the continent and elsewhere (BBC NEWS, August 16th, 2013). Good governance revolves around settling and harmonizing issues that cause economic and social collapse. However, growth must also be coupled with policies that deliberately attack poverty and promote and improve education, health and social safety nets. A credible and well-governed state builds enabling environments that generate economic growth and political stability thanks to the rule of law.

---

[24] http://www.whitehouse.gov/sites/default/files/docs/africa_strategy_2.pdf

When there is an erosion of public sector salaries, the quality of public services decline as well and teachers abandon their classrooms, nurses leave clinics unattended and offices stand empty while public servants turn to private trade in search of income for their livelihood in order to survive in the absence of sustainable social security safety net. In schools, children found themselves paying for supplies that once were freely provided; in hospitals, patients found it necessary to "tip" to secure a towel, a washcloth, or a bed pan. A bureaucracy that had been created to facilitate the lives of the citizens began instead to undermine their welfare. Its members began to feed themselves by consuming the time and money of those they once had served. The most visible of those endowed with the power to coerce was, of course, the military. Their salaries, too, eroded or fell into arrears. Their uniforms became tattered; the quality of food declined in their mess halls, and their equipment malfunctioned and, for want of funds, could not be repaired. Like doctors and nursing aides, they sold services to which the citizens were formally entitled (Bates 2008:45-46). As Kasozi (1994) states about Uganda in the mid-1980s,". . . any soldier who needed money would just pick an isolated part of the road, put logs or chains across it, and wait for unfortunate travellers. These twentieth-century highwaymen would rob everyone of anything they fancied: cash, watches, cassette radios, clothes, and the like." As a consequence of this, the armed forces responded by going on "looting sprees". As Lemarchand (2003) put it, they demolished downtown Kinshasa, the national capital, cordoning off commercial blocks, chasing shopkeepers from their premises, smashing windows, and carting off food, clothing furniture and appliances (Bates, 2008:104-106). Fragile states are plagued by two structural problems—political fragmentation and weak institutions—that together preclude the formation of any robust governing system, severely undermining the legitimacy of the state and leading to political disorders that are highly unstable and hard to reform and are often trapped in a cycle of violence.

CHAPTER II

Everything is About Security

Water constitutes one of the most important parts of the state strategy concept, regarding national security and statehood governance, sustainable development and food/livelihood resilience. Water is the only unconditional precious resource that all living things cannot do without. The availability of water resources often influences the level of sustainable food security, and socio-economic development in general. Water security is increasingly becoming a common concern with accelerating climate change, and in addition in the Near East and the Sahel regions, as a result of population growth. The more population grows, the more it affects the ecosystem resulting in environmental degradation, deforestation, which affects groundwater as well as water security. Since the beginning of civilization, nations and regions all over the world shared water in a form technically known as trans-boundary water management. However, the current pace of industrial development and population growth are pushing these natural resources to their extreme limits. Water resources have historical and emotional connotations and value, and can easily lead to tensions in countries and areas where there are asymmetric relations in the balance of power, both on the military and economic sides. The tension over water is often centred on the right to access and equity entitlement.

Kofi Annan asserted that ". . . unsustainable practices are woven deeply into the fabric of modern life. Land degradation threatens food security. Forest destruction threatens biodiversity existence. Water pollution threatens public health, and fierce competition for fresh water may well become a source of conflicts and wars in the future[25]." Water may trigger armed conflicts, and should be a common concern shared by all policymakers at all levels of leadership. This means that national security issues should not viewed in terms of the military balance of power according to traditional tunnel vision strategies; instead what is required is the capacity to plan ahead both at the national and sub-regional levels, and to cooperate with riparian states on trans-boundary water resource management.

Security factor

It is a basic elementary conceptual understanding. The fact that from livestock, watering holes and fertile land to trade routes, fish stocks and spices, sugar, oil, gold and other precious commodities, war has too often been the best way to secure possession of rare and valuable resources. Even today, the uninterrupted supply of fuel and minerals is a key element of geopolitical considerations[26]. In East Africa, in South Sudan in particular, the tensions between different communities constitute a major constraint upon the access to green pastures. Some rural communities, particularly the pastoral communities, are forced to leave the areas where they normally take their livestock to graze, and find themselves caught up in conflicts. Meanwhile, it becomes harder for them to find water for their cattle, and that makes them an easier target for cattle rustlers. Threats pose challenges to the management of water resources on the continent and to the satisfaction of competing demands for basic water supply and sanitation, food security, economic development, and environmental security. The crucial role of water in accomplishing the needed socio-economic development goals is widely recognized[27]. A study conducted

---

[25]   Collier-Hoeffler conflict model (1998) claims that Africa's natural endowments, such as diamonds, gold, copper, bauxite, and oil are strong predictors of violent conflict in Africa. The geographical locations, including the Nile river basin, are potential triggers of conflict in the horn of Africa. Majeed A Rahman; Water Security: Ethiopia-Egypt Transboundary Challenges over the Nile River Basin-*University of Wisconsin-Milwaukee.*

[26]   United Nations-Secretary-General New York, 17 April 2007

[27]   The Africa Water Vision for 2025: Equitable and Sustainable Use of Water for Socioeconomic Development

by the National Intelligence Council (2013) focused on several specific regional issues of certain rivers and water basins. Those included the Nile in Egypt, Sudan and nations further south, the Tigris and Euphrates in Iraq and the greater Middle East, the Mekong in China and Southeast Asia, the Jordan River that separates Israel and the West Bank from Jordan, the Indus and the Brahmaputra in India and South Asia as well as the Amu Darya in Central Asia. The study concluded that drought, floods and a lack of fresh water may cause significant global instability and conflicts in the coming decades, as developing countries scramble to meet demand from exploding populations while dealing with the effects of climate change. The risk of water issues causing wars in the next 10 years is minimal even as they create tensions within and between states and threaten to disrupt national and global food markets. The report estimated, however that beyond 2022, the use of water as a weapon of war or a tool of-terrorism will become more likely, particularly in South Asia, the Middle East and North Africa[28].

Environment factor

Environmental degradation might trigger conflicts, both intra and inter-states. Services should be valued in economic and financial terms. Unsustainable subsidies for agriculture should be replaced by cross-subsidies to enable the poor to get access to drinkable water and to reduce pollution of the already available water resources. Smakhtin (2002) defines environmental water requirements as the amount and quality of water required to protect an ecosystem to enable ecologically sustainable development and water resource utilization. Extreme changes in ecosystems may occur if water available for environmental uses falls below a certain threshold. Many countries are beginning to incorporate these concepts into their water resources management strategies to reserve a certain quantity of water for environmental or ecosystem uses. Water reserved for the environment can help regulate pollution and sustain the riparian ecosystem. Sufficient in-stream water availability can help to temper water pollution through the dilution of contaminants in the

---

[28]   National Intelligence Estimate on water security, which was requested by Secretary of State Hillary Rodham Clinton and completed last fall.

watercourse[29]. Moreover, water management needs to be conducted while keeping sustainability in mind. When that does not happen, water crises can emerge within a given region. As an FAO study in Northern Somalia showed, the country's water security has been worsened by the fact that for decades wells have been dug without a geo-hydrological study conducted by any governmental professional hydrologist body. The lack of governmental regulatory oversight eventually led to a depletion of the water reserves[30]. Environmental degradation, aggravated by climate change, has destabilizing effects on regions that are already conflict-prone, especially when it comes with inequitable access to scarce resources. The impacts are global and felt disproportionately by the poor, and that is why coordinated multilateral action to promote environmental sustainability is urgently required[31]. In North African and Middle Eastern countries, environmental stress caused by the presence of large populations, shortages of land and the scarcity of natural resources can all be linked to security concerns, as water is not available in quantities sufficient to meet the high demands that exist because of agricultural development and rapid urbanization[32]. The Intergovernmental Panel on Climate Change report estimated that by 2020, between 75 and 250 million of people are projected to be exposed to increased water stress due to climate change. By 2020, in some countries, yields from rain-fed agriculture could be reduced by up to 50%. Agricultural production, including access to food, is projected to be severely compromised in many African countries. This would further adversely affect food security and exacerbate malnutrition. The scale of the crisis in the Horn of Africa underscores the urgent need to better understand climate trends in the wider region and to identify

---

29   Mark W. Rosegrant, Ximing Cai and Sarah A. Cline, *World Water and Food to 2025: Dealing with Scarcity*, International Food Policy Research Institute, 2002-164

30   Somalia Water and Land Information Management (2013), *FAO study warns of depletion of Somalia's groundwater resources*, http://www.faoswalim.org/node/69

31   United Nations Report of the Secretary-General's High-Level Panel on System-Wide Coherence: Delivering as One (2006): A /61/583:

32   United Nations Secretary-General's High-Level Panel on Threats, Challenges and Change (2004) A/59/565:

areas where populations are most at risk from climate-related causes[33]. Environmental security addresses the consequences of environmental degradation, which include depletion of natural resources, such as water and land, where unwise developmental land use practices may contribute to societal, political or economic instability or conflict. Africa is the world's second-driest continent after Australia. According to the United Nations, 66% of Africa is arid or semi-arid and more than 300 of the 800 million people in Sub-Saharan live in a water-scarce environment less than 1,000 m^3 per capita per year. Africa's rising population is driving demand for water and degradation of water resources. Africa's population, excluding the northern-most states, is around 838 million and its average natural rate of increase is 2.6% per year, compared to the world average of 1.2%. It is estimated that the population will grow to 1,245 million by 2025 and to 2,069 million by 2050[34]. In August 2006, a huge toxic contamination affected the coast and waters of Ivory Coast, in the area surrounding Abidjan. The multinational company Trafigura, from the UK, voluntarily dumped toxic products there, seriously affecting water security, which in the end had repercussions on food security. As a result of this, an estimated 100,000 people sought medical treatment. Trafigura allegedly did this because disposing of the toxic products legally in the Netherlands would have cost too much, so they decided to get rid of the problem by polluting the coasts of Africa. Even though it has received a €1 million fine the company still denies any involvement in the incident[35]. According to them, the pollution has been caused by an Ivoirian company, adding that the people living in the area already suffered from water-related health problems long before the toxic waste dumps[36]. According to Greenpeace, this event showed "that a company can put a country into a medical crisis through toxic waste dumping, and still get away with it[37]". Nigeria is the

---

[33] International Organization for Migration (IOM) Office for the Coordination of Humanitarian Affairs (OCHA) United Nations University (UNU) and the Permanent Interstate Committee for Drought Control in the Sahel (CILSS)

[34] United Nations Millennium Summit in September 2000, Millennium Declaration.

[35] BBC News Africa (2010), Trafigura found guilty of exporting toxic waste,

[36] IRIN News, CÔTE D'IVOIRE: Scandale des déchets toxiques-A qui la faute

[37] Harvey F, The Guardian.com/environment-Septermber /25, 2012

top oil producer in Africa but in spite of that, it almost has no refineries capable to meet the needs for the refined oil product, petrol, for the demand of local consumption. In addition the country's oil transporting infrastructures are decades old and suffer from advanced decay. There are several consequences to this: oil leaks from the pipelines, contaminating waters usually used for domestic purposes, for agriculture, and eventually affecting the ecosystem, destroying the vegetation and killing tons of fish, which are of the utmost importance to keep a certain level of community livelihood and food security in the Niger Delta[38]. The big oil companies, such as Shell, say that pollution is due to acts of sabotage committed by uprooted young men whose hope is only to survive the strong wind of poverty and economic inequality. Nigeria is the most populated country in Africa, with a population of 150 million; it is also the second largest economy and largest oil exporter of the African continent. These three elements should have turned Nigeria into a leading regional power. While ordinary people are faced with societal challenges that cripple them with poverty and the lack of minimum social safety nets, men turn to illegal crude oil refining because they have no other means to generate income. This illegal industry gets support from transnational organized crime that has settled in the Niger Delta area[39]. Shell and other companies were criticized for having failed to maintain their infrastructures in a good shape and to prevent sabotage[40], and Shell has been found guilty in a Dutch Court of law, after Nigerian farmers sued the company for negligence[41].

The Rio+20 Conference focused on two critical themes: a green economy within the context of sustainable development and poverty eradication[42].

---

[38]   BBC News Africa, *Nigerian way of life under threat from pollution*, http://www.bbc.co.uk/news/world-africa

[39]   Al Jazeera and Agencies (2012), *Nigeria leaks billions from rampant oil theft*, http://www.aljazeera.com/video/africa

[40]   United Nations call for $1bn fund to clean up Nigeria oil spills, http://www.bbc.co.uk/news/world-africa-14413174

[41]   Smith-Park (2012), Farmers sue oil giant Shell over Niger Delta pollution, CNN/2012.Edition

[42]   United Nations Environmental Security Initiative, the Rio+20 conference

Destruction and over-exploitation of natural resources and ecosystems can threaten the security of communities and nations; instead good environmental governance and trans-boundary cooperation may provide a crucial pathway for stability, peace and sustainable livelihood building[43]. The achievement of development goals agreed upon internationally, including those contained in the Millennium Declaration, requires a new partnership between developed and developing countries. Water is fundamental for life, for socio-economic development and the conservation of ecosystems. In this regard, its sustainable management must be promoted while keeping in mind the objective of ensuring access to water for present and future generations, taking into account those internationally agreed development goals[44]. Conflicts affect environmental security with long-lasting consequences. The United Nations Development Program concluded in a February 2007 study regarding collateral damage inflicted on critical infrastructures that 7 out of 46 environmental issues investigated had a "severe" and "medium-term (1-10 years)" or "long-term (10-50 years)" impact on the environment. It includes: "littoral pollution from oil spill" considered to be "catastrophic"; impact on marine biodiversity from the Jiyeh power plant oil spill; "impact natural resources from quarrying", soil erosion from forest fires"; "loss of flora[45]". The Jiyeh power plant incident[46] had a detrimental impact on the environment in terms of solid and hazardous waste management; contamination of the soil and fresh water resources; weapons used; air pollution; and marine and coastal environment are concerned. Pollution occurred in each of these categories with potentially serious health risks for the local population[47]. While not related to a post-conflict situation, the Exxon Valdez Oil Spill in Alaska is another example of how an environmental crisis can affect

---

[43] Evaluation Environment and Security Initiative (ENVSEC) Report/2010

[44] Declaration of Santa Cruz. Cruz de la Sierra, Bolivia. 5 December 2006.

[45] Lebanon Oil Spill The Jiyeh power plant in Lebanon. Report, September 2006

[46] On July 14th 2006, the third day of the military conflict between Israel and Hezbollah, a rocket hit the fuel storage area of power station in Jiyeh causing over 20,000 tons of oil to spill into the Mediterranean Sea.

[47] United Nations Environment Program Post-Conflict Environmental Assessment Nations, January 2007

the ecosystem and the population on the medium to long term. Some fish population collapses did not occur until 3 years after the initial spill[48]. On the other hand, there is increasing evidence that environmental neglect, mismanagement and decline increase the probability of conflict and thereby pose a risk to human security. Unsustainable land management practices, environmental pollution and global atmospheric change are having significant impacts on human systems: for instance, improper mining practices bring the danger of hazardous waste spills and cross-border water pollution. According to the World Wildlife Fund, uncontrolled floods are the result of mismanaged rivers. In recent years, floods have become even worse than before and with ever more devastating effects. This is related to human mismanagement and climate change, both of which are believed to be linked to the fact that more extreme weather events are happening nowadays and are deadlier[49]. The 2001 Zambezi River Valley flood in Mozambique killed 700 people and displaced a quarter of a million. Still in Africa, experts have identified the reasons behind floods in the Limpopo River basin, including: heavy, episodic, localized rainfall, often associated with tropical cyclone activity and saturated soils from preceding events; land-clearing and poor agricultural land management in the upper river basin; associated soil erosion and increased runoff; and lack of integrated management of upstream dams and wetlands[50]. According to a World Health Organization report, the contributing factors are poverty, widening development gaps, the collapse of public health infrastructure, urbanization, civil strife, new use and development of biological products, environmental change and degradation, and globalization of travel and trade[51]. Although environmental stress is not directly responsible for political instability, it is often a contributing factor.

---

[48]   Exxon Valdez Oil Spill occurred on March 24, 1989 in Prince William Sound, Alaska. left thousands of birds and animals dead.

[49]   World Wildlife Fund, 28 August 2013

[50]   Amaral and Sommerhalder 2004; Leira *et al.*-2002.

[51]   WHO/global outbreak alert and response. report meeting Geneva, Switzerland/26-28 April 2000.

There is also considerable evidence that environmental cooperation helps to ease political tensions, and create an atmosphere of peace, stability and cooperation at all levels[52]. Conflicts may arise not only because of political and military threats to national sovereignty; they may derive also from environmental degradation and the pre-emption of development options. Conflict prevention is one of the bedrock-foundations of the Charter of the United Nations. The United Nations operations are globally focused on the need to address the socio-economic, cultural, environmental, institutional and structural causes that trigger food insecurity and poverty[53]. Moreover, we generally have a poor understanding of the nexus between environment and security, or to be more specific, between environment and violent conflicts. The sad thing is that this lack of understanding keeps the international community from developing adequate cooperative mechanisms aimed at conflict prevention and peace building. There is a need for more systematic assessment of the links between environment and security and a more careful consideration of the important links between environmental degradation/resources and development. The United Nations Secretary-General Ban Ki-Moon said: *"The environment has often remained the unpublicised victim of war. Water wells have been polluted, crops torched, forests cut down, soils poisoned, and animals killed to gain military advantage*[54]*"*. Yet the environment continues to suffer in times of war, threatening the well-being of vulnerable populations and undermining prospects for lasting peace. Nearly half the world's people—including the vast majority of the rural poor—directly rely on natural resources for their daily sustenance and income. If we are to achieve the Millennium Development Goals, and prevent competition over dwindling resources from contributing to new conflicts, we must acknowledge the critical role these resources play in maintaining peace. As global population increases and the demand for resources grow, the potential for conflicts over natural resources could intensify.

---

[52] United Nations Environment Programme/ Global Ministerial Environment Forum Nairobi, February,21-25 2005

[53] United Nations Secretary General, Report A/55/985-S/2001/574

[54] United Nations Secretary-General Ban Ki-Moon,6 November 2011

The impact of climate change may exacerbate these threats. In response, we will need to develop new ways of thinking on the sources of insecurity and ensure that our preventive diplomacy takes into account the trans-boundary nature of ecosystems and environmental degradation[55].

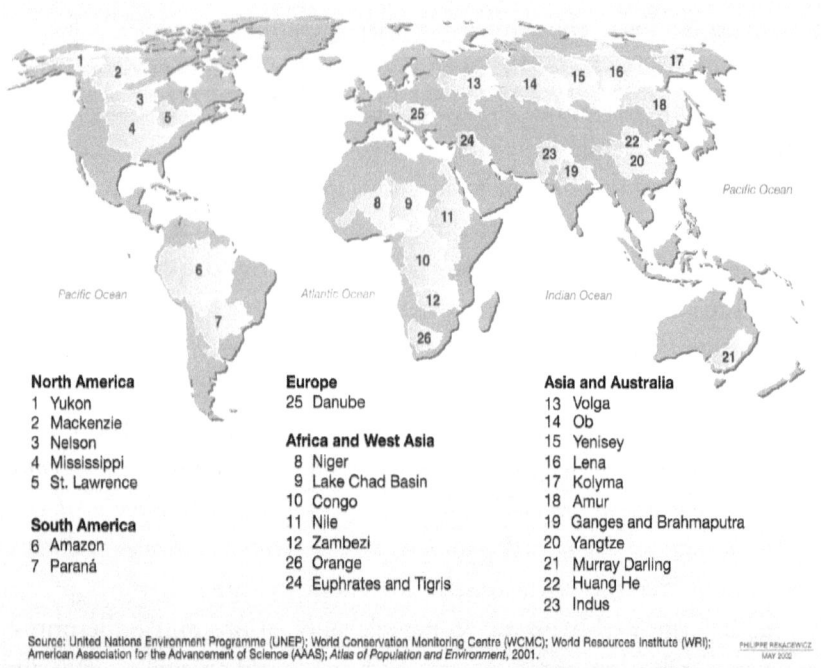

North America
1 Yukon
2 Mackenzie
3 Nelson
4 Mississippi
5 St. Lawrence

South America
6 Amazon
7 Paraná

Europe
25 Danube

Africa and West Asia
8 Niger
9 Lake Chad Basin
10 Congo
11 Nile
12 Zambezi
26 Orange
24 Euphrates and Tigris

Asia and Australia
13 Volga
14 Ob
15 Yenisey
16 Lena
17 Kolyma
18 Amur
19 Ganges and Brahmaputra
20 Yangtze
21 Murray Darling
22 Huang He
23 Indus

Source: United Nations Environment Programme (UNEP); World Conservation Monitoring Centre (WCMC); World Resources Institute (WRI); American Association for the Advancement of Science (AAAS); Atlas of Population and Environment, 2001.

Water does not recognize borders as it flows from one country to another. Any claim of the sole ownership of trans-boundary waters constitutes a violation of another state's rights.

In certain parts of Africa, water is in abundance and shared through international river basins, eventually creating a permanent interdependence among the nations part of those particular regions. Therefore any threat to the flow of water in these nations constitutes an International Security threat. The lack of water to sustain the demand of a population in need will leave the government with little choice but to take up arms to defend

---

[55]   United Nations Secretary General Ban Kin-Moon, 6 November 2010

its vital national security interests, provided that there are pre-existing multi-literal arrangements, which offer a safety net for member countries. There currently are international instruments, such as treaties, regional commissions and initiatives, governing the principle of equitable and reasonable utilization of trans-boundary waters. Water management legal experts call it the sub-set theory of limited territorial sovereignty. These agreements entitle each basin state to a reasonable and equitable share of water resources for its own beneficial use. However, the balance of interests must always be taken into consideration, because of the necessity to articulate the general needs with contemporary requirements, due to climate change and population growth: this explains why there is a need for those countries to establish multilateral agreements. The established principle of international water law has contributed greatly towards the creation of permanent bilateral and multilateral mechanisms aimed at streamlining water management systems and consultation mechanisms in Africa, Asia and the Middle East. These mechanisms imply that states in an international basin are allowed to use the water flowing in their territory in a manner that would not cause significant harm to the other basin states, including the environment and human and animal health and safety. This allows for consultation, negotiation and transparency between riparian states. Countries that are crossed by an international river are entitled to prior notice, cooperation and information exchange on every development project. Increased power production, accessibility and reliability, lead to economic growth and a better quality of life that are all of paramount importance in unstable areas. Enhanced watershed management leads to increased land productivity, food security and water conservation, as well as increased and good quality flows, resulting in an increase in tourism and allowing wildlife reproduce itself in a sustainable manner. Co-operation among the nations of the Nile Basin is meant to enable a mechanism to share substantial socioeconomic benefits, and promote regional peace and security, as highlighted in its founding principles, established in 1999, *of a shared vision to achieve "sustainable socioeconomic development through the equitable utilization of, and benefit from, the common shared water resources*[56]*".*

---

[56]   The NBI is governed by a Council of Ministers of Water Affairs

From 2003 to 2009, the equivalent of the Dead Sea, in stored freshwater volume, has vanished from the Tigris-Euphrates Basin. In May 2013, Israel announced that it would allow water to flow from the Sea of Galilee to the Jordan River, in order to avoid further tension. In 1994, the Araba Treaty was signed, installing peace between Israel and Jordan and normalizing their relations[57]. In 1999 however, because of severe droughts, Israel decided to reduce the amount of water provided to Jordan, which forced that country threaten to take retaliatory action. It took five weeks to resolve the issue, which ended with Jordan receiving the amount it was asking, according to what had been agreed in the 1994 treaty. As is the case concerning many other matters, the Israelis and Palestinians are often in a situation of disagreement regarding water[58]. Jordan and Syria agreed on a joint project to build a dam on the Yarmouk River, and subsequently built it[59]. The two countries had previously signed, in 1987, an agreement on the use of the Yarmouk river water, as well as the repartition of river generated electricity. Dams in Turkey have reduced water flow to Iraq and Syria by 80% and 40% respectively, since 1975. Since there are no international agreements between Turkey, Syria and Iraq regarding water resources, progress is hardly achievable. Furthermore, any progress is hindered by the internal armed conflicts in Syria and Iraq. Problems with water sharing emerged after the Ottoman Empire collapsed: before that, it was effectively managed, since the rivalry only appeared after States became sovereign. Since the 1960s and 70s, Syria and Iraq have repeatedly protested against various dam construction projects in Turkey.

---

[57] http://www.mfa.gov.il/mfa/foreignpolicy/peace/guide/pages/israel-jordan%20 peace%20treaty.aspx ; in article 6.3, both parties agree that their natural water sources are insufficient and that further ways to obtain water should be developed "through various methods, including projects of regional and international co-operation".

[58] http://www.water.gov.il/Hebrew/ people living in areas of water stress

[59] Ilan Berman and Paul Michael Wihbey: The New Water Politics of the Middle East (1999)

Equity factor

The Nile River has been the source of political tensions and low-intensity conflicts among three of its major riparian countries (Ethiopia, Sudan and Egypt). However, since the late 1990s, the Nile basin countries-with the encouragement and support of the international community—have made some attempts to establish basin-wide cooperative institutions. This process of engagement and collaboration is presently under severe stress due to increasing demand and decreasing supply of water resources in the basin. This situation may be further complicated by global climate change, which is anticipated to result in long-term changes in the volume and pattern of runoff in the Nile River system. Water is a natural endowment, but it can be considered as a non-renewable resource, and the existence of states is centred on access to water. Since the beginning of civilization, nations and regions all over the world shared waters technically known as trans-boundary water. However, in the distant past the need for water was different and its utilization was at a minimum, compared to the current pace of industrial development and population growth. Kofi Annan's point of view is the same we will come to in our conclusions: water may trigger armed conflicts in the future and should be a common concern shared by all the citizens of the world. Governments, when considering their national security in terms of military power regarding inter-state conflicts, should not view it in a traditional tunnel vision manner, but they should also have the capacity to plan ahead both at the national and sub-regional levels, and to cooperate equivocally with riparian states on trans-boundary water resources management. This will allow them to safeguard their national strategic security interests while mitigating the threat of a war over water problems[60].

The Horn of Africa has been always the theatre of destructive conflicts. Most of those have ceased but the conflicts have only been partially solved. Whereas the rest of these conflicts remain frozen or only cosmetically addressed, a small misstep could threaten the status quo of the fragile peace and security situation within the region, creating waves of societal

---

[60] Cam McGrath and Sonny Baraj "Water Wars Loom along the Nile" 2004 news 24.com 17.EPA North East Africa 2010 report

instabilities associated with armed conflicts. This can result in spill over effects, such as refugee crises in the receiving country, which is sometimes already struggling to cope with its own internal problems, such as economic and food security resilience. The majority of conflicts in the horn of Africa have been both interstate and intrastate conflicts. Undoubtedly, for several years the root cause of these destructive wars has been related to disputes over land and legitimacy. The first intra-state war in Kenya was because of contradicting claims over territorial jurisdiction and legitimacy, which led to the Shifta war of 1963-1967. The war was a consequence of secessionist attempts shortly after the Kenyan independence. These conflicts are mainly concentrated in the north-eastern and central Africa. While many of these have been caused by disputes over land occupation, mainly in oil rich areas of the Congo or in Sudan, others have been related to the issue of diverting precious water resources. Their exploitation requires adequate protection of the groundwater, which are of the utmost importance, and has to be based on sound hydrological, environmental, economic and social principles[61].

Ground water is interwoven with numerous other components of the physical environment and interacts with a large variety of human activities. Groundwater is linked to a hydrological cycle of various components[62]. Trans-boundary waters are some of the most economically important, highly stressed water sources, and are located in some of the most populated areas on earth[63]. The Nile River Basin consists of 11 countries and proposes that the international community immediately makes an effort to enact a comprehensive program as opposed to partial cooperation. Otherwise, the 300 million people who depend on the Nile will be confronted with even more profound challenges now and in the future. Two Nile river basin countries, Egypt and Sudan also form part of the Arab Region, one of the driest and most water stressed regions on Earth[64].

---

[61] Ofelia Tujchneider, Gregory Christelis Jac Vander Gun National University ElLitoral

[62] O. Tujchneideretal./EnvironmentalDevelopment7(2013)6-16 page 8;

[63] Alfred M. Duda a, n, Andrew C. Humeb a Former Senior Advisor, Global Environment Facility, Washington

[64] Jack T. Trevors, P. Weiler/EnvironmentalDevelopment7(2013)1-5-8

According to FAO by the year 2025, 1.8 billion people will be living in regions with water scarcity. The availability and quality of water in many regions of the world is increasingly threatened by overuse, misuse, pollution and projected negative impacts of climate change (FAO, 2013). According to a study in Water Resources Research, an American scientific journal, between 2003 and 2009 the region that stretches from eastern Turkey to western Iran lost 144 cubic kilometres of fresh water. It is equivalent in volume to the Dead Sea and according to the study's senior author Jay Famiglietti, of the University of California, the region is suffering the world's second-fastest rate of water depletion after northern India. The water table sank by 0.3 metres (one foot) a year from 2006 to 2009. Along the Tigris and Euphrates Rivers, Turkey and Syria could currently be approaching a massive confrontation over water resources. The Tigris-Euphrates Basin—located in the Fertile Crescent that gave birth to agriculture itself, is steadily getting drier. At the point where the Euphrates crosses from Syria into Iraq, it now flows at only 70% of the rate it once did. All this happens in an area that already faces severe water shortages[65]. Water stress syndrome and shortages are common among nations sharing this precious resource, raising tensions at the national, regional and international levels between organizations and require the implementation solutions to allow for better freshwater management systems.

Unresolved water-related equity problems will contribute to instability, in particular in areas where the balance of power is not obvious, in terms of economic and military power. Oil was used in the Middle East producing countries as an instrument against Israel and its Western allies in 1973, which resulted in a global economic crisis. From a socio-economic point of view, Africa felt this crisis more than any other region in the world due to the endemic poverty and underdevelopment as consequence of weak economic performance in the postcolonial period. Social scientists argue that Sub-Saharan Africa's economic performance has been poor and has worsened, since the oil crisis of the mid-1970s. Water security management and water equity issues remain open to consultations with all the stakeholders. In the Middle East, water resources are plummeting.

---

[65] The Economist The waters of Babylon are running dry March 9th 2013

While it has 5% of the total world population, the Middle East & North Africa (MENA) region contains only 0.9% of the global water resources. The number of water-scarce countries in the Middle East and North Africa has risen from 3 in 1955 (Bahrain, Jordan and Kuwait) to 11 by 1990 (with the inclusion of Algeria, Israel and the Occupied Territories, Qatar, Saudi Arabia, Somalia, Tunisia, the United Arab Emirates and Yemen). Another 7 are anticipated to join the list by 2025 (Egypt, Ethiopia, Iran, Libya, Morocco, Oman and Syria)[66]. On the African continent, the Nile River is of the utmost important for the livelihood of millions of people as it is often the only fresh water source in regions suffering from extreme weather conditions and advanced desertification. Human security in Sub-Saharan countries can be said to have two main aspects: firstly, safety from chronic threats, such as hunger, disease and repression; secondly, it means protection from sudden and harmful disruptions in the patterns of daily life—whether domestically, at work or in communities (Michael E. Brown, et al 2004:251-2). The demand for food is expected to rise by at least 35% by 2030, while demand for water is expected to rise by 4%. Nearly half of the world's population will live in areas experiencing severe water stress.

Demography factor

Demographic constraint is constituted by rapid population growth and urbanization, resulting in increasing demand on scarce resources under conditions of limited managerial capacity.

A related factor is the high prevalence of communicable diseases and premature death due to inadequate, unsafe and inequitable access to water supply and sanitation. Countries need to review the trade-offs between different population policies in order to ensure that demographic factors do not limit socio-economic development or lead to increased water scarcity. The threats of climate change are real; its impacts are being felt in the Sahel region and in North Africa. The major environmental factor is climate variability leading to drought, desertification, floods and other natural disasters. At the national and international levels, this is absolutely

---

[66] The New Water Politics of the-Middle East. http://www.iasps.org/strategic/water. htm

critical for Africa's sustainable social and economic development. If they are not addressed, the impact of climate change related issues is going to affect the food production capacity of the local communities. To resolve this problem, multi-lateral institutional cooperation is required to enable governments to promote effective trans-boundary water management and economic cooperation and integration for mutual benefit. In particular supporting emerging countries or those facing sporadic armed conflicts and security instability should be a priority, since those issues greatly increase the risk that they end up facing food shortages. Countries like Somalia and Mali face multiple and complex crises, droughts on one hand and armed conflicts and political instability on the other. Crises like these are the drivers of food insecurity. Climate change is having a great impact on nations that are politically and economically insecure and unable to stand by themselves without external cooperation and support due to weak institutions of governance. These assumptions must be better analysed through the lenses of a new horizon of economic development opportunities. In recent years, Ethiopia showed some leadership agility, successfully seizing opportunities in Africa. For example when most of Sub-Saharan National Airlines were left on the ground and went bankrupt, Ethiopia Airlines became the only inter-continental company to take advantage of this huge emerging market. The new leadership agility consists in taking advantage of the multi-polar world where the new emerging powers, such as the BRICS, and China in particular, are offering unconditional opportunities to enable sustainable economic development. The new Ethiopian leadership understands and acknowledges that drought cannot be prevented because it is a natural phenomenon. Its effects however, such as famine, are preventable thanks to a structural food security and resilience policy that has to be established by the governments. The decision taken by the government of Ethiopia to build the Grand Renaissance Dam is a clear indication of how determined the people of Ethiopia are. They are determined to safe-guard their national security interests through the construction of a critical strategic infrastructure. In East Africa, no country knows better than the Ethiopian government the impact of weak food efficiency in terms of production, the consequence of which is millions of deaths. The Ethiopian leadership does not want to have to fight against famine again in their country, like it happened before in the 1970s and 1980s. Water is becoming a national issue that no state seems to give-up on. Ethiopia's late Prime Minister, Meles Zenawi, made the following declaration: "—*Some people in Egypt have old-fashioned ideas based on the assumption that the Nile water belongs to Egypt, and that Egypt has a right to decide who gets what, and that the upper countries are unable to use the Nile water because they will be unstable and they will be poor. These circumstances have changed and changed forever* [67]*."*

Economically the country is making impressive progress with steady growth, and on the military front it is also involved in high profile peacekeeping and security stabilization forces. Concerns have been raised by international organizations, including the United Nations, on how to deal with shared water management through multilateral coordinated efforts. It was impossible in the past as individual states used every instrument of power to serve their own interests, disregarding all the other nations. The vast majority of East African Nations are emerging economies. The governments of the Nile Basin are in constant pressure to deliver good services, all these requiring sufficient waters resources. The construction of strategic infrastructure, such as irrigation channels and dams can be the source of future tensions. The demographic power of the Nile Basin: the United Nations estimated recently that the total population stands at 457 million, representing the equivalent of 44% of Africa's total population. About 54% of the population living in the Nile Basin riparian countries depend on water from the river, which represents 238 million people, i.e. 24% of Africa's total population. FAO and CIA World Fact-Book forecasted that, by 2030 the total number of people living in the Nile Basin area could reach 336,080,000[68]. In the past water equity was not fully addressed in terms of distribution. Those days are over though: in terms of demographic power, Ethiopia is the most populated country in the region with over 90 million, bypassing Egypt which has 85 million. By mid-2011, Africa's population, excluding the northernmost states, was around 838 million and its average natural rate of increase was 2.6% per year, while in the rest

---

[67] *The Egyptian Gazette* 20 May 2010: Ashok Swain-Challenges for Water Sharing in the Nile Basin: Changing Geo-Politics and Changing Climate: Hydrological Science Journal, vol 56, no.4. 2011,pp.687-702

[68] Nile Basin Initiative, http://nilebasin.org

of the world has an average rate of 1.2%. Between 2009 and 2050, the world population is expected to increase by 2.3 billion, from 6.8 to 9.1 billion (UNDESA, 2009*a*). At the same time, urban populations are projected to increase by 2.9 billion, from 3.4 billion in 2009 to 6.3 billion total in 2050, (UN-Habitat 2006). At the regional level, Ethiopia is increasingly becoming a major power in the horn of Africa. Demographically, the country's population has overtaken the population of Egypt. Its economic growth averages 10.7 per cent. In 2012, Ethiopia was the 12th fastest growing economy in the World. By 2025 it could attain middle income status, according to an Ethiopia Economic Update report[69]. Ethiopia's grand renaissance dam on the Blue Nile River is a reflection of the shift in the balance of power within the region. Egyptian leaders often use different means including diplomatic leverage on multilateral institutions to discourage Ethiopia from engaging in projects that are regarded as a threat to national security interests embedded in the Nile Rivers. Ethiopia's first priority is to maintain its security, and thus prefers that Egypt would not to take retaliatory measures against it, but is trying to gain a portion of the vast amount of the water that originates in its territory. Ethiopia would also want Sudan to cooperate although it currently enjoys good relations with its members. Sudan has good relations with Egypt, although they are strained at times as Sudan periodically regrets the fact that it does not get a fair share of water from the Nile, compared to its northern neighbour. Ethiopia has vowed to engage Egypt over the control of water resources in the Nile valley basin. Egypt's response to a statement made by Kenya's assistant foreign affairs minister when Mohammed Abu Zeid, Egypt's minister for water resources, remarked that Kenya's statements were a "declaration of war" against Egypt and subsequently threatened an economic and political embargo of Kenya. This looming tension among riparian countries is further worsened by Kenya's continuing threat of engagement for new measures. In 2002, a senior Kenyan minister, Raila Odinga, called for the review and renegotiation of the 1929 treaty, which gave Egypt the right to veto construction projects

---

[69] Michael Geiger, World Bank's Country Economist for Ethiopia. The Economic Update is the 2nd report launched this fiscal year and is a key element of the World Banks' Ethiopia Economic Update-Laying the Foundation for Achieving Middle Income Status, ADDIS ABABA-June 18, 2013.

on the Nile river basin, and said "it was signed on behalf of governments which were not in existence at that time.; promote self-sustaining development, collective self-reliance, the interdependence of member states regarding national and regional strategies[70]. Sub-regional institutions encourage and forge above all a strategic framework that allows for a better understanding of the factors that might create conflict, one of them being that cooperation regarding the sharing of water, if not addressed at the earliest, could result in a conflict. In this context, it appears that diplomacy led by activism aiming at an acceleration of consultations and trying to facilitate inclusive consultations, negotiations and decision-making processes at the highest level, whereby directives are implemented systematically at all levels of governance, seems to be the best way to act. Nile Basin States acknowledge that sustainable shared water management is of paramount importance to their national security, in the long run, and can eventually effect the enhancement of food security. Through a joint cooperation states are able to maximise their output and able to achieve long terms sustainable water, and ultimately food, security[71]. The Ethiopian Government has decided to finance the project by selling Government bonds[72]. The neighbouring states began showing many interests Djibouti, one of Ethiopia's neighbours, sent a $1 million cheque to help building the dam. Djibouti already purchases electricity from Ethiopia, and the new dam would mean more electricity for Djibouti at a cheaper price. Ethiopia's Grand Renaissance Dam on the Blue Nile River is a reflection of the shift in the balance of power within the region. The changing geopolitical situation has provided alternative possibilities for Ethiopia and Sudan to raise finance and technical support on their own initiative water related developmental projects. The Grand Renaissance Dam project has been on the drawing board since the 1960s, but it was not until March 2011 that Ethiopia officially declared its intention to carry out the construction.

---

[70] The Southern African Development Co-ordination Conference, SADCC, the forerunner of the SADC, the Community, was established in April 1980 by Governments of the nine Southern African countries of Angola, Botswana, Lesotho, Malawi, Mozambique, Swaziland, Tanzania, Zambia and Zimbabwe.

[71] Ashok Swain-Hydrological Sciences Journal-Journal des Sciences Hydrologiques, 56(4) 2011 687-692

[72] *Grand Renaissance Dam Bond Well Under Sale*, April 2013,

Ethiopia and Egypt have agreed to review the impact of the Grand Renaissance Dam even if they still have radically different opinions about the project. Ethiopia would like to develop some kind of win-win strategy with. The late Ethiopian prime minister said in that regard that "the past is a past based on a zero-sum game[73]." Nile Basin States acknowledge that sustainable shared water management is of paramount importance to national strategic security interests in the long run, and can eventually enhancement of food production capacity[74]. According to the Mekong2Rio Conference, by 2040 there will be another two billion people on the planet so, given the challenges from climate change and rapid urbanization, the pressure on water, energy and food is growing, and the world faces increasing challenges to resource availability, management and sustainability. When these resources cross international and state boundaries, their management becomes more complex, calling for greater cooperation and involving a wider range of actors[75]. Trans-boundary water resources management principles have been established and recognized by international conventions, and international treaties, thereby reinforcing the theory of limited territorial sovereignty. Trans-boundary water sharing involves interstate cooperation between upstream and downstream countries, and need to include mutual rights and duties in their use, and each is entitled to an equitable share of its benefits. Equitable and reasonable utilization rests on a base of shared sovereignty and equality of rights. However it is generally acknowledged that it does not necessarily mean that shared waters cannot necessarily be shared equitably, strictly speaking. It entails a balance of interests that accommodates the needs and uses of each riparian state. This is a principle established by international water regulations and has substantial support in practice, along with judicial decisions and international codifications.

---

[73] Ethiopia *National Security* Ethiopia/ Grand Renaissance Dam Project. *http://www. aljazeera.com/news/middleeast/2011/09/2011917132445980153.html*

[74] Ashok Swain-Hydrological Sciences Journal-Journal des Sciences Hydrologiques, 56(4) 2011 687-692

[75] Mekong2Rio: International Conference on Trans-boundary River Basin Management, 1-3 May 2012, Phuket, Thailand.

Water is a silent weapon that influences countries to change their behaviour, which often occurs when a country is threatened with military mobilization. In May 1975, Syria closed its airspace to Iraq over a water dispute; after the latter had threatened to bomb the dam the former was building. There was no direct violent conflict thanks to the mediation led by Saudi Arabia[76]. Turkey is similar to Egypt regarding the use of water, although their actual geostrategic positions differ greatly from one another. However in terms of political, economic and diplomatic influences both countries enjoy a good level of support of the international community. Egypt controls water coming from a river that does not originate on its territory, while the Euphrates and Tigris both have their sources in Turkey. The most likely source of political and social unrest in the Middle East over the next twenty years is not warfare or military coups—it is over water. Ten of the fifteen driest countries in the world are in the Middle East, and agricultural policies in the region are depleting already scarce groundwater reserves at an alarming rate. If this process continues, it will undermine the strength of governments that tout their control over water as a sign of political success. Conventional security threats dominate the public debate and governmental thinking, but water is a true game-changer in Middle Eastern politics.

International frameworks on water management provide guidelines on trans-boundary water distribution. They provide the principles of equitable and reasonable utilization and the standards of obligation and of not causing significant harm to ecosystems. Furthermore, they give principles of cooperation, of notification, of consultation and for the peaceful settlement of disputes. The Okavango Basin has one of the most varied savannah woodlands and wetland ecosystems in the whole world. This river originates in the rainy highlands of Angola, runs through Namibia for about 2000 km and flows into the Okavango Delta in Botswana. The livelihood of the inhabitants of these three countries depends on the efficiency and effectiveness of the trans-boundary basin water management system. Securitization in the Okavango River Basin has aggravated

---

[76]   Aaron T. Wolf and Joshua T. Newton, *Case Study of Transboundary Dispute Resolution: the Tigris-Euphrates basin*, Institute for water and watersheds, Program in Water Conflict Management and Transformation,

tensions between the riparian states by heightening perceptions that access to water depends more on its use or misuse by neighbouring states than on domestic consumption or on the vagaries of nature. This reveals how securitization leads to policy responses informed by a desire to protect the "here" from the "elsewhere". Securitization in the Okavango River Basin involves the political, military and economic powers, as well as the societal and environmental sectors. ". . . due to massive deforestation and loss in surface vegetation, flooding now annually occurs in some areas, such as in the banks of the Blue Nile River and in the vast plains of the Baro Akobo Basin in the country's South-western region. Although sometimes associated with economic and social damages, floods provide much needed water to ensure the fertility of graze-lands, making them anticipated events, especially for nomads, whose incomes are dependent on animal husbandry. In general, human society has positioned itself in areas with locally sustainable water supplies, in the form of runoff, and/or river and stream flows . . ." (Strzepek, K. et al, 2001).

The Mekong contains the world's largest fresh water capture fishery with about 2.3 million tonnes per year. Aquaculture is increasing fast, particularly in the Vietnam Delta, where it has risen from 200,000 to 2 million tonnes per year. Until recently, human interventions have had little impact on the river's regime. The Mekong River remains one of the most bio-diverse rivers in the world, second only to the Amazon. The river's annual flood pulse continues to support a rich natural fishery and an extensive and unique wetland environment. The Mekong River and its tributaries sustain tens of millions of people in Southeast Asia. Rice farmers also depend on water and sediment from the river to irrigate and fertilize their crops. A predicted rise in sea level will increase salinity and floods in the Mekong Delta, causing damage to crops in the most productive area of the basin[77]. The European Union committed 4.95 million euros to the Mekong River Commission in order to enable an adequate response to the climate change challenges in the region. "Water feeds, nourishes, moves, powers and

---

[77] *Luang Prabang,* European Union (EU); Mekong River Commission (MRC)-challenges. http://www.mrcmekong.org/news-and-events/news/the-european-union-provides-over-6-million-usd-to-tackle-climate-change-in-the-mekong/ *Lao PDR, 16 January 2013.*

heals"[78]. The objective of the conference was to address the trans-boundary dimension of the water, energy and food security nexus with particular emphasis on the challenges that rapid human-made developments and environmental change pose to the sustainable management of trans-boundary river basins[79]". The sustainable management of water resources is the key to people's lives and the development of society.

The tripartite water sharing situation involving Syria, Iraq and Turkey remains unsolved, and it is highly unlikely to be for a while due to instability in two of these countries. The key to solving water scarcity issues for Iraq and Syria resides in the optimization of water storage during the winter. Of course, water scarcity strongly impacts the agriculture, which in turn can severely affect food security, and, among other sectors, the economy. As for the Israeli-Palestinian situation, just like the rest of the questions involving those parties it is a very complicated issue, currently unsolved, and it will remain unlikely to be solved until a solution to the problems beyond water is found. The Middle East is one of the most water insecure regions in the world. This already scarce natural resource has the potential to spark conflict throughout this troubled region. Indeed, the importance of the latter is reinforced by the fact that many of the region's central waterways are shared by several riparian states. In this respect, the most likely sources of inter-state water conflicts are the Nile, the Tigris-Euphrates and the Jordan River basins.

All of these potential sites of conflict involve several countries. Yet, despite the scarcity of water throughout the Middle East, there have been surprisingly few military conflicts between disputing parties. The most likely reason for the absence of "water wars" is that in each potential case, there has always been one party that clearly has the upper hand in terms of diplomatic, military and economic power. The importance of good governance is that it provides for self-regulated institutions the opportunity to build an environment where political stability and rule of law become a

---

[78]   International conference on trans-boundary river basin management, Phuket, Thailand, 1-3 May 2012, http://www.mrcmekong.org/news-and-events/events/mekong2rio/?url=/mekong2rio/

[79]   Mekong River Commission, *Trans-boundary River Basin Management*

source of mutual benefits between those who are governed and those who rule. The main water basins in the region are Lake Chad and the Niger, Senegal and Gambia Rivers. The Niger River basin is Africa's third largest after the Nile and Congo, and is shared by no less than 11 countries. Major lakes in the region include Lake Faguibine in Mali, Kainji Lake in Nigeria, Lake Volta in Ghana and Lake Chad, which borders Chad, Nigeria, Niger and Cameroon. Groundwater resources range from shallow aquifers that are refilled seasonally to ancient sedimentary water basins, which are non-renewable and difficult to access, reaching depths of up to 2,000 meters.

The importance of good governance is that it provides for self-regulated institutions the opportunity to build an environment where political stability and rule of law become a source of mutual benefits between those who are governed and those who rule. They are embedded in soft and hard power. Indeed all kinds of powers vary from time to time. However all that remains is the tangible elements that constitute power itself. The people and their willingness to support certain ventures for sustainable common interests is what matters. The relation between national security and national solidarity in the horn of Africa has never been greater than now. In the context of national security more people within the region are becoming aware that everything and anything is possible with the people' support both spiritually and economically. Armed conflicts in the horn of Africa have been the drivers of the current status quo in certain countries. Ethiopia has always been embroiled into interstates and intrastate wars. Most of the time, Ethiopia has been at war. The longest interstate war between Eritrea and Ethiopia lasted 30 years, causing human and physical resources drain to Ethiopia in particular, along with the combination of natural phenomena such as drought causing famine. Water and environmental security are the part and parcel of sustainable development and as a result of food security. Water resources constitute the most important element of food security. Food security and economic development depend on the quality and availability of fresh water endowment. Water is a common resource, shared among nations between upstream and downstream countries. The preciousness and the scarcity of water are placed on the list of every community, nation, and region, because of its importance. One should not forget that water is life.

Sharing water should be the fundamental strategic imperative of survival, for each individual, community, government or regional institution. Water cannot be controlled or monopolized by one nation alone; any such attempt in these modern times is counter-productive due to the demands towards development that every single nation is yearning for. Ethiopia is arguing that it has a complete sovereign right to exploit the waters that flow within its territory. This includes utilizing Nile waters in a reasonable and equitable manner even if there is a decrease in the quantity and quality of flow into Sudan and Egypt (Bulto, 2009). Some commentators argue that as a result of geographic and political changes, under these circumstances there could be an "open conflict over water" in the Nile Basin (Brunnée and Toope, 2002). According to international law, a riparian country must provide the other riparian countries with an advance notice of uses or changes in existing uses that include a risk of significant harm, together with relevant technical information, and also obliges riparian countries to consult with one another about any new use or change in existing uses. As an upstream riparian country that has not made much use of the Nile, Ethiopia initially balked at the idea of having to notify and consult with countries like Sudan and Egypt before using water from the portion of the Nile that flows through Ethiopian territory. Ethiopia also pointed to the fact that Egypt had never given notice of its planned projects, even though it later pointed to them as existing uses that could not be harmed by Ethiopia's new uses. In addition, as part of the negotiation process, Ethiopian officials were made to understand that prior notification was, and is, a well-established, fundamental principle of international law. Sudan, South Sudan and now Egypt have recently been undergoing unusually strong political turmoil, and only time will tell when they are ready, willing and able to focus on the Nile again. All to say that rather than continue to pull back, now is the time for the international community to redouble its efforts to move towards a new Nile River Basin-wide comprehensive governance regime, marked by cooperation and joint management of trans-boundary resources, in contradiction to one of only partial cooperation and unilateralism which might well dominate the Nile River Basin for the decades to come. In spite of the international community's support for cooperative water management of the Nile water, it has not been able to take a foothold, and most of the basin countries, particularly Ethiopia,

Sudan and Egypt, have undertaken unilateral actions to protect their water interests. The changing geo-political situation has provided alternative possibilities for Ethiopia and Sudan to raise financial and technical support for their own water development projects. Meanwhile, Egypt has lost some of its bargaining power, is limited with the changing nature of the world today. In the Middle East there are fragmented and vulnerable links in the management of water between most of the countries. The lack of international credible framework to oversee trans-boundary water management with the current stress might increase the likelihood of self-help schemes and eventually lead to future conflicts. Sharing water is a strategic imperative of survival. In order to avoid open conflicts, the only solution under international law is consultation: riparian countries need to consult with one another about any new use or change in existing uses. The international community, and the United Nations in particular with its comparative advantages, have a role play to resolve the question of water equity in the Nile River Basin, a question that dates back to before the independence of upstream countries with the exception of Ethiopia. The current veto power exercised by Egypt cannot be sustainable given the national dynamics and the global trends. Therefore it is imperative for the international community to facilitate a comprehensive integration of governance regimes, marked by cooperation and joint management of trans-boundary resources including the reviewing the historical rights which grant veto powers to the detriment of other nations. Riparian states need to develop 'no regrets' options for water planning and management that are socially and economically viable over a range of possible climate futures. Water resources constitute the most important element of food security. Food security and economic development depend on the quality and availability of fresh water endowment. The preciousness and the scarcity of water are placed on the list of every community, nation, and region. One should always keep in mind that water is life. Any attempt to monopolize water resources heightens tensions that could eventually become contributing factors to a potential armed conflict.

It is therefore imperative for the international community to facilitate the integration of trans-boundary water governance institutions and to revise old agreements that prevent some countries from using rivers flowing through their territories and to improve cooperation over trans-boundary water management thus encouraging international consensus in adequately addressing water equity. Trans-boundary cooperation where water stress is prevalent, such as in the horn of Africa and in the Middle East, is a lasting solution for sustainable peace and security. Fragmentation in the integrated management of water resources dashes any hope of achieving basin-based management in the near future, and at the same time have increases the possibilities of open dispute among the riparian countries.

CHAPTER III

Interdependence, Vulnerabilities and Risks

Transnational Organized Crime

The era of globalization provides opportunities for both economic and intellectual development but it also creates, at the same time, a "global vulnerability". Global organized crime is the world's fastest growing business, with profits estimated at $870 billion in 2009[80]. In Europe, in Asia, in Africa and in America, the forces of darkness are at work and no society is spared. Traditional crime organizations have, in a very short time, successfully adapted to the new international context to become veritable crime multinational companies. Illegality is thus corrupting entire sectors of the international activity. The danger is all the more pernicious as organized crime does not always confront the State directly. It becomes enmeshed in the institutional machinery. It infiltrates the State apparatus, so as to gain the indirect complicity of government officials[81]. Leaders around the world are very much aware of the impacts and the consequences that transnational organized crime can cause to their local economies and to their people. Elias Jassan, then Secretary of Justice of Argentina, said that organized crime was "a new monster", while Silvio Berlusconi said those organizations were "armies of evil" who could be defeated "only by

---

[80]   United Nations Office on Drugs and Crime, *Estimating Illicit Financial Flows Resulting from Drug Trafficking and Other Transnational Organized Crimes: Research Report* (Vienna, October 2011), www.unodc.org/documents/data-and-analysis/Studies/Illicit_financial_flows_2011_web.pdf

[81]   Boutros Boutros-Ghali, World Ministerial Conference on Organized Transnational Crime. Boutros Boutros-Ghali, Secretary-General, United Nations. World Ministerial Conference in Naples, Calls for Effective International Action against. `Crime Multinationals, United Nations, Naples, 21-23 November 1994

international collaboration[82]". Argentina's senior leadership understands the impacts of organized crime in Latin America in general.

The impacts of narco-trafficking originating from Colombia and Mexico have been the driving force for years of destabilizations in these countries, combining drug and terrorism problems. For example, the FARC in Colombia have used criminal modi operandi. Silvio Berlusconi requires no one to explain to him how destructive organized crime can be to a dynamic and vibrant society. The Italian Mafia has been the negative driving force that has for years undermined the Italian institutions of governance, as well as both private and public sectors by polluting the country's vital organs of legitimacy and state administration. **The Italian Mafia had a** thriving industrial life whose networks could include high profile representatives of every level of the political system—politicians being influenced; the economic system—influencing businessmen and undermining fair deals; the criminal justice system—prosecutors and lawyers on their payroll; and the law enforcement systems. Social protection for workers, union leaders and other officials could also be compromised at a certain point by the influence of organized crime elements. Any attacks on critical infrastructures, such as oil pipelines, the kidnapping of international expatriates in the Sahel region and the penetration of international Islamist radicalisms and extremism is a threat-to-national, regional and international security therefore constitute a security challenges. It no longer comes from a small number of powerful and hostile states but from multitudes of unknown, invisible non-state actors, such as transnational organized criminal syndicates and terrorist groups who easily seek sanctuary in failed, weak and/or fragile states. Moreover, other factors contribute to this instability. Statehood functional holes are thus exploited by transnational organized criminal networks and terrorist groups because of the existence of this vacuum of security. The legitimacy deficit in some areas resulted in the creation of illegal quasi-governments operated by the aforementioned groups. In some instances, government corruption undermines the efforts to defeat criminal activities. Drug traffickers from

---

[82]   Following the United Nations Secretary General's speech, several speakers reaffirmed the need for more international cooperation in order to address the issue of transnational organized crime.

Colombia and Venezuela are linked to senior officers in Guinea Bissau and Guinea Conakry[83]. Corruption is one of the drivers of statehood fragility due to the fact that some states are plagued by two structural problems— political fragmentation and perpetually weak national institutions—that together preclude the formation of any robust governing system that is transparent, severely undermining the legitimacy of the state and leading to political orders that are highly unstable and hard to reform. The political fragmentation directly impinges on the ability of countries to foster the positive institutional environment necessary to encourage productive economic and social behaviour because it undermines the usefulness of traditional informal institutional systems and squanders built-up social capital, while disabling attempts to construct robust formal governing bodies. The net result is societies with low levels of interpersonal trust and extraordinarily high transaction costs.

A Boeing 727 from Venezuela carrying an estimated five to nine tonnes of cocaine landed at Tarkint, near the city of Gao in northeast Mali, in November 2009. It unloaded its cargo and made a failed take-off attempt, and was then set alight. The drugs were never recovered. An investigation revealed that a Lebanese family and a Mauritanian businessman who had made a fortune from Angolan diamonds were among the backers of the enterprise. How could such a large plane carrying so much cocaine freely enter a region that, although desert, was neither uninhabited nor ungoverned[84]? While officials originally thought the plane had crashed,

---

[83]   CONAKRY, 10 October 2008 (IRIN)-Guinea has become a major drug-trafficking hub and the trade there is now potentially more dangerous than in Guinea-Bissau, according to Antonio Mazzitelli, regional representative of the UN Office on Drugs and Crime. Though the amount of drugs trafficked through Guinea is unclear, OCAD's new head, Sakho Moussa Camara, told IRIN over 1,000kg were seized in Guinea in 2007. He said the office has seized 7,499kg of drugs between 19 August and 15 September 2008.

[84]   Serge Daniel (Agency France Press)-Dec 11, 2009, Burnout Boeing, a clue in African drugs trade. The burnt out wreck of a Boeing 727 lies abandoned in the Sahara desert, what is left of it covered by a little more ochre sand every day. United Nations officials say the plane landed in the remote northeastern area of Mali in West Africa in early November with a load of cocaine and other illegal goods from Venezuela in South America.

investigators believe that the plane was burnt deliberately after it had landed and the cocaine had been removed. In 2010, a Malian police commissioner was convicted in connection with attempts to build an airstrip in the desert for future landings. In places where governmental security authorities have no footprint and influence at the local level, the issue of corruption can be widespread. This has a deeply corrosive effect on the people's trust in their government and contributes to the rise of crime and political disorder. In the political realm, corruption undermines democracy and good governance by flouting or even subverting formal processes. For example, the former caretaker President of Guinea-Bissau has been linked to a major cocaine and arms trafficking scheme allegedly run by a former senior military officer from the small and unstable West African state. According to prosecutors, he planned to bring 3.5 tonnes of Colombian cocaine to the African country inside a shipment of military uniforms and then smuggle weapons, including surface-to-air missiles, back to Colombia's FARC rebels[85]. With the country's economic prospects limited to the few within a state where economic benefits are as rare as the hen's teeth, senior public servants find themselves in a situation of poverty. Chronic political crises have put Guinea Bissau in a state of economic stagnation and paralysis for decades. Guinea Bissau has experienced constant constitutional order disruptions and as a consequence, the institutions of governance have degenerated into a state of anarchy and chaos, creating safe passages and havens for transnational organized crime groups. While other countries in West Africa are moving forward through democratization and institutional development in line with the current pace of the post-cold war world, for Guinea Bissau this progress is unrealistic and cannot be achieved without the support of an external force. Guinea Bissau may be an ungoverned space, becoming the starting point of the Arc of instability and chronic institutional crisis, posing challenges from the Gulf of Guinea to the Gulf of Aden, two locations that pose regional security threats. Guinea Bissau is the virtual consequence of the phenomenon of statehood governance failure. The reality is that "Failed States" pose a security challenge both to national, sub-regional, regional and international security interests.

---

[85] Admiral Jose Americo Bubo Na Tchuto a former Chief of the Guinea-Bissau navy was caught in a Drug Enforcement Agency (DEA) sting operation on board a yacht in international waters in the Atlantic in early April 2013,

Politically and economically, Guinea Bissau requires reconstruction and rehabilitation. Its weakness dates back to the 1970s, back to the post-colonial independence political leadership. Since then the country has witnessed the emergence of a political leadership class of activists competing for power grabbing through unconstitutional means, until the point where it undermined good democratic statehood governance on the pretext of protecting national sovereignty and integrity. Statehood collapse in the Horn of Africa, particularly in Somalia, can be considered a failure: along with the collapse of the state came the complete disintegration of the institutions of governance. The images of insecurity associated with the term "failed state" are often ones of violence and complete anarchy, economic stagnation, poverty and weak security governance that lead to lawlessness. Guinea Bissau is tangled in a deep crisis, and the hard task that consists in resolving it is beyond its means. Economically, politically and institutionally, the country cannot stand on its feet alone, without external support. According to the former Executive Director of UNODC, Antonio Maria Costa, "drug cartels buy more than real estate, banks and businesses; they buy elections, candidates and parties. In a word they buy power: corruption in legislative bodies reduces accountability and undermines policymaking; corruption in the judiciary compromises the rule of law; while corruption in public administration results in poor social equality[86]". Romano Prodi, former Italian Prime Minister and the United Nations Secretary General's Special Envoy to Sahel Region, writes: "It's simple, without regional strategy there is no hope of development. With the regional strategy there is hope to link the Sahel to the new, promising Africa. Africa's Sahel, which stretches from the Atlantic Ocean to the Red Sea and includes Chad, Mali, Mauritania, Niger and parts of Sudan, Cameroon and Nigeria. The region faces a complex of problems that include not only political instability, most notably in Mali, but also endemic poverty, lack of resources and infrastructure, porous borders that allow trafficking of all kinds, and multiple human rights issues"[87]. West African governments, including those of Ghana, Nigeria, Guinea

---

[86]   Charlie Edwards, Senior Research Fellow/Director National Security and Resilience, the Crime Terror nexus in West Africa RUSI Analysis-15 May 2013

[87]   http://www.un.org/apps/news/newsmakers.asp?NewsID=91. *Interview with Romano Prodi, Special Envoy of the Secretary-General for the Sahel*

Bissau, Guinea Conakry, Gambia and Mali, are struggling in their efforts to provide adequate common goods in large parts of their territories due to multifaceted institutional weaknesses severely affecting all aspects of human security. The danger is that transnational organized criminal networks exploit areas of state weakness, in particular those linked to the management of the public common good. These include security and basic social food safety nets. The combination of poverty, underdevelopment, and chronic insecurity are the perfect storm to create incentives for unlawful elements and their illegal behaviour. At the same time, simplistic law enforcement measures can and frequently do further degrade human security. These pernicious dynamics become especially severe in a context of violent conflict. The problems linked to the situation in post-Gaddafi Libya is that they are becoming complex, as some of them are recurring and unresolved issues coming from unequal representation allowing for discrimination and threatening peaceful coexistence. There are expressed concerns at the national, sub-regional, regional and international levels regarding the consequences of the hard drugs penetrating the societal fabric of the region. At the local level, the civil society is playing a vital role in sounding the alarm over the coming danger if drug trafficking ever becomes normalised in Western African societies. The lessons learned from Colombia and Mexico have accelerated the understanding of the threat and raised risk awareness amongst all stakeholders, policymakers, think tank institutions and pressure groups. They have joined their efforts to promote public awareness, thereby enabling institutional commitment regarding the implications of inaction, in order to deal with drug trafficking in a systematic and coordinated manner at the local, national and regional levels. The Kofi Annan Foundation launched the Commission on the Impact of Drug Trafficking on Governance, Security, and Development in West Africa. The mission will be headed and chaired by former president of Nigeria General Olusegun Obasanjo. At the launching of the commission Kofi Annan said: "*The massive surge in drug trafficking in West Africa over the last decade presents a serious and growing threat to the region's stability and development. Left unchecked, illegal drug trafficking could compromise the encouraging progress that West African nations have made in strengthening democracy and promoting human and economic development. We have seen what has happened in other parts of the world where it has destabilized societies corrupted the system and brought incredible violence. And of course we don't want to see that happen here and the idea is for us to look at the issue critically, get the evidence and make recommendations for action*[88]. To resolve the drug problem in Western Africa, a new pragmatic approach on part of those who need to fill in to compensate for the states' lack of reaction capacity. The governments have the obligation to ensure that there are mechanisms put in place to make security governance a reality in these territories. According to the former secretary general of the United Nations Kofi Annan, there is solution to the current problem. This solution entails that: "Only when government is grounded in the rule of law—fairly and consistently applied—can society rest on a solid foundation. Leaders must ensure that the rules are respected—that they protect the rights and property of individual citizens. Leaders must also hold themselves to the same rules, the same restraints—never above them[89]". Cooperation is necessary to address this phenomenon, and the United Nations are working closely with the authorities in Côte d'Ivoire, Guinea-Bissau, Liberia and Sierra Leone in the context of the West African instability.

The effects of the Libya crisis are better understood by looking at the agility of Al-Qaida in the Islamic Maghreb and how it begun to form alliances with drug traffickers and other criminal networks. These alliances have potential to become the destabilizing driver of regional security. West Africa is also becoming a transit route for drugs which are destined to the European cocaine market, with an estimated value of $900 million annually[90]. The South American drug cartels are exploiting regional security governance vulnerabilities in the region to diversify their shipping routes

---

[88]   Former President of Nigeria, Olusegun Obasanjo, chaired high level body on growing threat to regional stability Accra. On 31 January-Former United Nations Secretary-General Kofi Annan today unveils a major new initiative to help tackle the growing threat from illegal drug trafficking in West Africa. The West Africa Commission on the Impact of Drugs on Governance, Security and Development (WACD) is being launched today at the Kofi Annan Peacekeeping Centre in Accra, Ghana. January 2013. http://kofiannanfoundation.org/newsroom/press/2013/01/kofi-annan-launches-west-africa-commission-drugs

[89]   Address by Kofi Annan, The Fifth Nelson Mandela Annual Lecture, July 2007

[90]   UNODC, 2013 report.

and to obtain new weapons for their fight against the authorities in Latin America. In West Africa, extreme poverty, unemployment, lack of border control, weakness of law enforcement state institutions structures, and corruption all contributed to create a perfect opportunity for transnational criminal groups to thrive and make more profits. Strategically, by the virtue of its geo-location, for the South American drug cartels and their local partners, West Africa represents not only the shortest, but also the most cost-effective channel to smuggle illicit drugs into Western Europe. Apart from the drug problems, there is also an increasing number of piracy incidents in West Africa. Trafficking in human beings, arms, and counterfeit medicines have also been reported, are growing, and are posing new security risks for policy-makers. As trillions of dollars of investments, capital flows, goods and services make their way around the world economy, so do at almost equal speed, people, ideas, consumer fashions, and rebellions against globalization and its impacts. The ever closer linking of economies, political and social communities has been fuelled by a revolution in technology and communications. West Africa is becoming one of the hubs of globalization's side-effects. International led threats require multidimensional efforts. Most regions affected by terrorism and transnational organized crime have a system in place that is ineffective, inadequate and ill-funded. The West Africa and Sahel region problems are multidimensional in their nature and scope, which include weak-statehood governance, systematic corruption and indiscriminate violence against innocent people. Those problems contribute to the spread of illicit weapons and drug trafficking, piracy and terrorist activities in a cross-section of fragile countries already struggling to overcome the consequences of years of civil war and instability. In his opening remarks, UN Secretary-General Ban Ki-moon said that "organized crime, drug trafficking and piracy were on the rise in the region and that last year's upheaval in Libya had sparked an influx of weapons. Diplomats from the region called specifically for the Security Council and the wider international community to help them identify and root out terrorist groups, such as AQIM which is allegedly involved in trafficking and other illegal activities throughout the region, and Boko Haram, which carries out deadly attacks in northern Nigeria. Samuel P. Huntington wrote: "Changes undermine traditional sources of political authority and traditional political institutions; they enormously complicate the problems of creating new bases of political associations and new political institutions combining legitimacy and effectiveness. The rates of social mobilization and the expansion of political participation are high; the rates of political organization are low; the result is political instability and disorder" (Huntington, 1968:5). There is a grave danger to national security when negative non-state actors, such as religious fundamentalists or extremists, and transnational organized crime forge an alliance in order to gain more competitive advantages, seeking to influence government decisions and to create an environment of lawlessness and anarchy. Joseph Nye referred to the effects of this kind of alliance as an "asymmetric interdependence". The symmetric relations of dependence and independence among states are different[91]. This applies to the triple alliances within the Sahel region, where major religious extremists are associated with terrorists groups and transnational organized crime to exploit structural and non-structural vulnerabilities.

In the Western parts of the Sahel region, countries constantly suffer from political and institutional crises as a consequence of constitutional order disruptions and of the lack of the smooth succession of power. The connection between terrorism and transnational organized crime in the Sahel region and West Africa in particular are the product of four things: lust for power, societal interests, position, and natural needs. All these have contributed to what can be easily perceived as the West African self-perpetuated human tragedy of institutional and internal security governance crisis. Violent conflict and constant deadly quarrels contribute to the culture of systematic uncertainties in which survival is the only prospect, at least for the short-term. Violent conflicts can be asymmetric in their nature because they exploit innocent civilians and encompass exploitative social relations that cause unnecessary sufferings. Since these security threats pose challenges to the global order, they require multilevel mitigating measures. The policy-making process in the Sahel region is a dynamic game among actors that interact in what can be positive steps for all stakeholders in search for a common goal and role to play for the betterment of national and international interests. There are

---

[91]   Joseph S. Nye, *Power and Interdependence,* 2d ed. (New York: Harper-Collins,-1989).

both positive and negative actors operating effectively within the region. The positive actors are subdivided into two categories namely: informal and formal. Formal positive actors form part of operational institutions of governance and state bureaucratic machines, such as police forces, justice and political with moral power and accountability. The informal positive actors include private business communities, social movements and the media. Negative actors pose political, security and economic risks in the region because some of the trends have been persistent over the past decades and remain one of the main concerns. These include economic downturn as a result of political instability and institutional crises. The challenges are multi-dimensional.

The majority of the Sahel countries are fragile states because they face severe chronic political instability and development challenges: weak institutional capacity and poor governance, as well as on-going violence. Weak governance also means low human capacity, and so low physical control of capital state resources, ultimately depriving the government of the necessary human capital to provide adequate public goods, security, and basic social services[92]. West African governments should work together in a joint effort to strengthen the security building capacity in order to achieve a better protection of the coastal waters. The Gulf of Guinea Commission made steps toward fighting piracy—ministers managed to make steps that can find in a gradual and strategic way to combat piracy, armed robbery and all illicit acts that currently harass, with growing peril, the Gulf of Guinea[93]".

The good intentions of regional leaders should not be turned into rhetoric of good policy and strategic frameworks at the regional level without the means to implement them as this could solely end up as vainglory. The security strategy should focus on the current crisis in Guinea Bissau. Guinea Bissau has been embroiled into political and institutional crises that have

---

[92]   http://www.oecd.org/development/incaf/38368714.pdf

[93]   Cândido Van-Dúnem (2013) Minister of Defence Gulf of Guinea Commission made steps toward fighting piracy. Established in 1999, the Gulf of Guinea Commission groups Angola, Cameroon, DR Congo, Republic of Congo, Nigeria, São Tomé and Príncipe, Gabon and Equatorial Guinea.

brought in international actors such as the United Nations and African sub-regional and regional actors. Political instability and institutional crisis in this country has paved the way for weak security governance in terms of law and order. The police and national defence forces, as guarantors of national security and territorial integrity in particular, are severely under-resourced, unable do their jobs effectively and efficiently for the common good.

There are weak links in the security governance and security and risk management of Guinea Bissau, given the political environment under which the current government is acting.

This is a concern of the utmost importance because the slightest weak link in security governance in a West African country will have negative impacts and consequences on the entire coastal area of the Gulf of Guinea. While the 'spoiler' behaviour on part of the country's elite and officials is partly an expression of legitimate political competition, it is also symptomatic of pervasive corruption in Sub-Saharan Africa. The general instability in the country makes it harder to achieve a democratization process because of the efforts to prevent it by senior members of the military forces. This incursion of the military into the governance process prevents a smooth evolution of the democratic process. Had it not been for this interference, the country could have potentially been revived, economically and institutionally, creating a precedent for the whole region.

Transnational terrorism

What exactly is transnational terrorism? The definition of terrorism is one of the most contested concepts of modern times. The differences and tensions that prevented the adoption of an official definition of terrorism lies in the fact that some people or a group considered as terrorists by one state could be considered as freedom fighters[94] by another, enjoying

---

[94] Arab convention on the suppression of terrorism signed at Cairo on 22 April 1998 on its preamble reads: the right of peoples

official recognition and legitimacy of their actions[95]. The definition of terrorism in this context regards terrorist acts as intentional acts, which may seriously damage a country, an intergovernmental or international organization such as the United Nations, for example. The strategic aim of international terrorists is to intimidate the populations or to compel governments to act in a certain way[96]. Terror is used by terrorist groups as a means to achieve certain goals, which can be driven by ideology, religious beliefs a need for political change or a way to fight for the independence of a region or country. Ever since the tragic 9.11 attacks and thanks to the strong influence of the media, terrorism has been associated with extremist religious groups. However, a quick glance at the global security situation will reveal that other kinds of terrorist groups still exist on all continents. And this multiplicity is also reflected in the presence of various definitions of what terrorism and terrorist acts are. Here is, for instance, the definition given by the Arab countries on the matter: "any act or threat of violence, whatever its motives or purposes, that occurs in the advancement of an individual or collective criminal agenda and seeking to sow panic among people, causing fear by harming them, or placing their lives, liberty or security in danger, or seeking to cause damage to the environment or to public or private installations or property or to occupying or seizing them, or seeking to jeopardize national resources[97]". Mohammed Khazaee wrote: *"terrorist acts constitute a flagrant violation of human right to life, leading to the lack of the full enjoyment of human rights and fundamental freedom of peoples. Such acts endanger the territorial integrity and stability of states as well as national, regional and international security, destabilize legitimated constituted governments or prevailing constitutional order and political unity of states, affect the stability of nations and the very basis of societies create adverse consequences on the economic and social development and cause the*

---

[95] Jorri Duursma of Terrorism and-Self-Determination. Harvard International Reviews, December 20, 2008

[96] United Nations Security Council resolution 1373, call upon all states to refrain from providing assistance to terrorist groups.

[97] *The Arab Convention on the Suppression of Terrorism. 22 April 1998.*

destruction of State[98]". According to the African Union, a terrorist act is defined as: "any act which is a violation of the criminal laws of a State Party and which may endanger the life, physical integrity or freedom of, or cause serious injury or death to, any person, any number or group of persons or causes or may cause damage to public or private property, natural resources, environmental or cultural heritage and is calculated or intended to intimidate, put in fear, force, coerce or induce any government, body, institution, the general public or any segment thereof, to do or abstain from doing any act, or to adopt or abandon a particular standpoint, or to act according to certain principles; or disrupt any public service, the delivery of any essential service to the public or to create a public emergency; or create general insurrection in a State. Any promotion, sponsoring, contribution to, command, aid, incitement, encouragement, attempt, threat, conspiracy, organizing, or procurement of any person, with the intent to commit any act referred to previously. The definition given by the Organization of the Islamic Conference reads as follows: "Terrorism means any act of violence or threat thereof notwithstanding its motives or intentions perpetrated to carry out an individual or collective criminal plan with the aim of terrorizing people or threatening to harm them or imperilling their lives, honour, freedoms, security or rights or exposing the environment or any facility or public or private property to hazards or occupying or seizing them, or endangering a national resource, or international facilities, or threatening the stability, territorial integrity, political unity or sovereignty of independent States"[99]. Since the end of the Cold War, global security depends on how to engage and interact with weak and failing societies, and encouraging economic, political, legal, and social change within them. Non-state actors are now among the greatest threats to security, and foreign policymakers must work with other non-state actors to meet the economic, political, and social challenges that underlie these new security threats. Since 1991, there are several areas where the security situation can be labelled as "hot peace". In those places, escalating community conflicts, guerrilla violence, and regional wars have or still do occur, resulting in

---

[98]   Ambassador Mohammed Khazaee. On behalf of the Non-Aligned Movement-, New York, 3 October 2011.

[99]   Convention of the on Combating International Terrorism, adopted at Ouagadougou, July 1999.

great loss of lives and in the destruction of the institutions of government, civil society, and private sector. This is particularly true in Asia, Africa, the Middle East and Latin America. More than one-third of the nations in the world are directly or indirectly affected by conflicts, political instability and institutional crisis. In the basket of risks there are two fundamental threats that are threatening security at all levels. Terrorism and organized crime have greatly contributed to the fact that the post-Cold War world is now characterized by many statehood vulnerabilities. Robert R Fowler writes: "Their objective was to establish a 7,000 km wide caliphate, stretching from Nouakchott in Mauritania to Mogadishu in Somalia, to be ruled by stern Allah-fearing Islamic sages who could be relied upon to understand and execute God's will. AQIM believe that by replicating across the Sahel the chaos and anarchy caused by their Al Shabaab colleagues in present day Somalia, they will be creating the perfect growth medium in which their vision will flourish."

The threat to the stability of the northern half of Africa posed by militant jihadi Islam is present and real. It has been exacerbated by the fall-out from our Libyan adventure, which has caused weapons in untold quantities to spew across one of the most fragile parts of the world. Not only do Al Qaeda's predations endanger the development gains of the past half-century in the upper part of Africa, but chaos there will very directly impact Western Europe as human emergencies of immense proportion bloom, and illegal refugee flows multiply by orders of magnitude. Our African friends need help to defeat such a scourge[100]." The Kenyan tourism sector has suffered from severe disruption due to a series of terrorist attacks and kidnappings of foreigners. This has taken a huge toll on the tourism industry, which is the most important of the country's economy. Those tragic events could alter the international general opinion that Kenya is a

---

[100] Robert R Fowler (2013) My 130 days in the hands of al-Qaeda's African "monsters", by former hostage. In July 2008, the United Nations Secretary General Ban Ki-Moon appointed Robert Fowler a former Canadian ambassador, as the Secretary General Special Envoy to Niger tasked helping to find a solution to the Tuareg conflict in the Agadez region in the north of the country. In mid-December 2008 he and his aid were kidnapped by the terrorists elements affiliated to Al Qaeda released on April 2009.

safe destination for tourists, and that is something the political leadership would never like to see happen. A loss of international confidence would result in a smaller number of tourists, which ultimately means a smaller flow of foreign currency, more unemployment and less tax revenue for the government.

On August 7th 1998, the terrorist bombing of the United States embassy in Nairobi left 80 people dead and more than 600 injured[101]. A few years later, two terrorist attacks targeted an Israeli plane and an Israeli owned hotel[102]. Both those attacks happened on November 28th 2002. While the missiles fired at the plane fortunately missed their target, the hotel suicide bombing resulted in the deaths of nine Kenyans and three Israelis. Meanwhile, the growing threats of kidnappings targeting tourists and foreign workers, as well as the occasional terrorist attacks, all show that there are some deficiencies in terms of security governance in Kenya. These deficiencies are made even worse by the presence of a security weak link in the region: Somalia's rebels and terrorists often retreat or even attack on Kenyan soil, meaning that Kenya's internal security will be at stake as long as Somalia's statehood failure is not addressed. The current multilateral arrangements to control international armed violence, terrorism, and political instability are inappropriate to deal with present and foreseeable by-product conflicts and threats facing vulnerable people of the countries in Africa, Asia and in the Middle East. Despite the fact that regional and international initiatives exist to address the issue of terrorism in those vulnerable places, the threat in the Sahel region has become too big to resolve without multilateral cooperation. However, it should also be noted that in order to achieve the intended results, the countries should implement adequate regional mitigating measures to deter terrorist groups from recruiting, acquiring

---

[101] August 8, 1998 http://www.theguardian.com/israel/page/0,850553,00.html

[102] Dan Williams Israeli Plane Countermeasures May Have Stopped Missiles, November 29th, 2002 Terrorists make an almost simultaneous attempt to shoot down an Israeli passenger jet taking off from Mombasa.

weapons[103], financing their operations, thanks to tightened cross border controls in a coherent and coordinated manner[104].

The national, regional and international instruments against terrorism are aimed at suppressing acts of terrorism with a preventive strategy that includes the fight against the promotion, sponsoring, contribution to, command, control, funding, publicizing, incitement, encouragement, threat, conspiracy, organizing, networking, procurement of explosives and technology used to commit acts of terrorism. The United Nations Security Council resolutions 1373 (2001) and 1624 (2005) are the bedrock foundation for the United Nations Member States to prevent terrorist acts both within their borders and across regions worldwide[105]. The global project offers a counter-terrorism strategy that facilitates sustained, tailor-made and specialized assistance to practitioners in their investigation, prosecution of terrorist offenders, as well as their expertise in capacity-building aimed at strengthening cooperation among states and regions[106]. The threat of terrorism is not static—it is constantly changing as global dynamics change[107]. "Terrorism still remains a threat to international peace and security as well as to economic and social development, making the world still vulnerable to acts of terrorist organizations that are constantly adopting new tactics and using new technologies available in the black markets. Terrorism in the Sahel region is likely to grow due to number of variables. Experts argue that countries that are prone to armed conflicts

---

[103] Counter-Terrorism Committee Executive Directorate (CTED) Concept note States in the Sahel region to strengthen their capacity in the global fight against terrorism. *New York, 20 September 2013*

[104] United Nations Security Council resolution 1963 (2010) encourages the Counter-Terrorism Committee (CTC) and its Executive Directorate (CTED) to continue to arrange meetings with Member States and relevant international, regional and sub-regional organizations on thematic or regional issues relevant to the implementation of resolutions 1373 (2001) and 1624 (2005).

[105] Security-Council resolution 1373 (2001)/Security Council resolution 1624 (2005).

[106] United Nations Security Council resolution 1373 (2001), prioritize is assistance and assistance

[107] United Nations G A Global Counter-Terrorism Strategy Resolution adopted by the on 8 September 2006 *(A/60/L.62)]* 60/288.

situations are likely become the breeding ground for the recruitment and spread of terrorism ideology, when states lack the capacity to address this phenomenon[108]. The holistic and comprehensive approach to counter terrorism has to include local communities, the civil society, and the media as well as the private sector and humanitarian organizations[109]. According to the Commonwealth of Independent States, terrorism should be combated in all its manifestations through international and national legal instruments, and therefore should be punishable under national and international criminal law. There is an urgent need for the international community to cooperate on these issues[110]. Heads of States and Governments in South Asia have already recognized the seriousness of the problem and agreed to cooperate to fight it[111], as did American States in the prevention and punishment of terrorism in general with a strong focus on kidnappings and murders[112].

No entity is immune to acts of terrorism, especially since the 9/11 attacks. After those tragic events, there has been an increase of attacks against international organizations, foreign States representatives, Humanitarian, Relief organizations and other non-governmental organizations. Critical infrastructures, such as bridges or power plants, have also been targeted by terrorist attacks thus contributing to further destabilization in fragile regions or states. On June 19th 2013, a United Nations compound suffered a truck-bomb attack that killed 13 people, the militant group responsibility for the attack calling the United Nations "a merchant of death[113]". On

---

[108] *Jean-Paul Laborde, Executive Director of the United Nations Security Council Counter-Terrorism Committee. Washington DC.*

[109] United Nations Security Council resolution 1963 (2010),

[110] Treaty on Cooperation among the States Members of the Commonwealth of Independent States in Combating Terrorism, 1999 at Minsk on 4 June 1999 Independent States.

[111] -Regional Convention on-suppression of Terrorism at-Dhaka Summit-of-December 7-8-1986.

[112] American States Multilateral Convention to prevent and punish the acts of terrorism extortion concluded at Washington on 2 February 1977.

[113] The United Nations expanded its presence this year, about 18 months after Islamic insurgents were pushed from the seaside city.

August 19th 2003, the United Nations headquarters, located in the Canal Hotel in Baghdad, suffered a devastating bomb attack. The detonation resulted in the death of 22 United Nations staff and visitors, and over 150 persons were injured[114]. International terrorism has evolved to become even more vicious. This new kind of terrorism is adapted to our globalized and interconnected world. This "technological terrorism" uses nuclear, radiological, chemical or bacteriological weapons or, pathogenic micro-organisms, radioactive substances as well as other substances that are harmful to human health. Roshandel and Chadha wrote: *After they left Afghanistan, the now emboldened mujahidin—also called jihadists—fanned out across the world. Some went back home where they worked to overthrow the local regime in order to install an Islamic Government; other went to free other Muslim lands, what choice was made often depended on where the best action was. In short, jihad had gone global* (Roshandel and Chadha 2005:37). The most high profile terrorist activities began in the 1970s when terrorists began to use aircraft hijacking. For instance, in December 1973, Arab terrorists killed thirty-two people in Rome's airport during an attack on a US aircraft.

---

[114]   Report of The Independent Panel on the Safety and Security of UN Personnel in Iraq 20 October 2003

Fig.: Understanding terrorism

KINDS OF ATTACKS :
  Suicide bombings; Kidnappings; Hostage taking; Drive-by shootings;
  Targeted assassinations
TARGETS :
  Public gatherings; Journalists; Humanitarian workers ; Tourists;
  Diplomatic mission representations
WEAPONS USED :
  Car bombs; Shoulder-fired missiles; Dirty bombs; Anthrax ; Airplanes as
  missiles
GOALS SOUGHT:
  Political demands; Freeing of prisoners; Morale boost; Publicity; Other
  demands
GROUPS:
  Nationalists; Religious; Radical militants

Source: Karen A. Mingst (2004:213)

On December 17th 1996, the Ad hoc Committee was established by resolution 51/210 of the General Assembly. The committee was created in order to establish international conventions to fight, and eventually suppress, a range of terrorism related acts, such as bombings or (nuclear) proliferation, thus eliminating international terrorism[115]. All policymakers in the world agree that only by joint efforts through multilateral cooperation at every level can they help to make the fight against terrorism and terrorist acts a successful one. Thanks to the development and expansion of the new technologies of communication, the world is now moving at great speed, with an ever increasing global interconnectedness that produced a culture of interdependence—meaning, essentially, reciprocal effects resulting from ties among different actors.

---

[115] The resolution established a committee to monitor the implementation of the measures mentioned in the resolution 1373

Both state and non-state actors are interconnected for specific dimensions, and by virtue of this connectedness have reciprocal impacts on one another, (Graham Allison 2000:72-3).

There is a new prototype kind of terrorism that uses a "copycat strategy". It has emanated from Iraq and is widely used in many regions. A giant country such as Nigeria is fighting against religious fanatics, extremists and radical fundamentalists driven by unrealistic views of religious dogma. The destructive nature of the copycat terrorism practised by those groups is behind the destruction of the good deeds accomplished by humble followers of Islam who, for centuries, had contributed to the cohabitation with their Christian brothers for the common good of the Nigerian people. Extremism and fundamentalism are difficult to deal with. It is however highly important to recognize the importance of the "driving soul force" behind the attacks they commit. This force is responsible for the destruction of innocent lives killed in the bombings, but also the lives of those whose mind has been twisted to push them to commit suicide attacks against other human targets, killing their enemies in exchange for the celestial paradise that their doctrine is said to offer.

The perfect storm

Different kinds of kidnapping threats can be found around the world: kidnapping for ransom; kidnapping with political elements and demands; and kidnapping by pirates. Countries where the threat of kidnapping is particularly prevalent, and where DFAT's travel advisories specifically warn of the threat of kidnapping, are: Afghanistan, Algeria, Bangladesh, Burkina Faso, Cameroon, Chad, Colombia, Democratic Republic of the Congo, Egypt, Eritrea, Ethiopia, India, Iraq, Kenya, Libya, Mali, Mauritania, Morocco, Niger, Nigeria, Pakistan, Peru, the Philippines, Saudi Arabia, Senegal, Somalia, South Sudan, Sudan, Tunisia, Yemen and the Indian Ocean, especially near the coast of Somalia. The instability that led to the international intervention in Mali has increased the risk of kidnapping throughout North and West Africa. Malian-based militants and others located in Nigeria and Niger have carried out a number of kidnappings over the past 12 months, including in neighbouring countries such as

Cameroon. Further kidnappings are likely in the North and West Africa region. Kidnapping cases differ in the motivations of the kidnappers, the demands being made for the release of the hostages, and the circumstances where the kidnapping has occurred. Terrorist and criminal groups both use kidnapping as a tactic to achieve their goals. Terrorist groups often target foreigners. In some instances, terrorists have killed their kidnap victims when their demands were not met. Foreign employees, particularly those in the oil and mining sectors, aid and humanitarian workers, journalists, tourists and expatriates are regularly targeted. Terrorists may use local merchants such as tour and transport operators to identify foreign visitors for potential kidnap operations. Hostages may be taken by their captors into a neighbouring country. Humanitarian workers and tourists in Kenya have been kidnapped by militants and held in Somalia. Pirates have kidnapped hundreds of people, usually holding them for ransom. Pirates have attacked all forms of shipping, including commercial vessels and pleasure boats. In South America, Colombia has one of the highest rates of kidnappings in the world, often perpetrated by FARC and National Liberation Army (ELN) in rural areas. Criminal groups often kidnap tourists who are forced to withdraw money from ATMs. This is known as "express kidnapping". It is common in countries in Central and South America, especially Mexico and Colombia, but does occur in other countries. In some cases victims have been killed or injured while attempting to resist the kidnappers. The use of ATMs located inside banks, hotels and shopping centres during daylight hours may reduce the risk. Some criminals pose as unlicensed taxi drivers. There are elements that make organized crime successful. Where there are weak institutions of governance, bureaucrats do not serve the interests of the people, instead using the state authority to create business schemes for their own benefit. The lack of accountability and oversight mentioned in the previous chapters are the incentives that drive transnational organized criminal networks towards the weak or failed states, where they can thrive, generating massive profits while undermining legitimate governments and their rights to collect taxes. The triple alliance between terrorist groups, local criminal elements and international crime syndicates constitutes a grave danger to national security governance in general, and this is especially the case in poor nations and developing countries whose security governance has weak links. Violent conflicts and political instability represent a "gold mine" for transnational crime groups, particularly in West and Central Africa, two regions where gold, diamonds, coltan, and timber, among others, are available in vast amounts. The profits were used to finance war theatres by bypassing international sanctions and armed embargoes in order to maintain the instability. This has been the case in Angola, the Democratic Republic of Congo, Sierra Leone and Central African Republic. The border issues problem is the center of the gravity of the security governance challenges facing the countries of the Sahel area: they are vast and porous, which makes effective patrolling extremely difficult. The lack of resources and cooperation makes it difficult for governments to address the issue. According to the United Nations Secretary General Report "on the situation in the Sahel region", It was estimated that in 2012 alone, the equivalent of 18 tons of cocaine, amounting to $1.25 billion, transited through West Africa, a portion of which allegedly passed through the Sahel. Apart from the lack of economic benefits and opportunities there is limited regional cooperation among states in the fight against terrorism and organized crime[116]. Kidnapping threats have been prevalent in the Sahel region for decades: tourists, foreign workers, diplomats, engineers, aid camps have been kidnapped. The objective in most cases was to obtain a ransom in exchange for the release of the hostages. The ransom money is then used to finance the illegal activities of the groups that commit these kidnappings. Kidnapping is one of the easiest ways to obtain money. For instance, ransom money "played a key role [in allowing the rebellion] to annex most of northern Mali. The money also feds, clothed and armed soldiers and paid bribes for local tribes" (David Cohen US Treasury Official, February 24th 2013). The security problems are increasingly becoming intertwined and widely connected to many sets of variables. This can create a situation where one security threat in one part of the region can quickly become one in another. The result of the Libyan revolution endangered the national security of Mali because dangerous weapons were stolen from the bases of Gaddafi's army. These weapons ended up in the hands of well-trained, disciplined and experienced terrorist fighters in the Sahel region. The collapse of Libyan security institutions came at the worst

---

[116]   United Nations-Secretary-General Report on the situation in the Sahel region

time possible, since the whole region was suffering from droughts that made the economic hardship even worse. A rebellion in northern Mali led by heavily armed Tuareg rebel groups and Jihad fighters, together with weak governance in Bamako, corruption, and an ineffectual counterterrorism response, culminated in the March 2012 coup d'état. Terrorist and extremist groups, including al-Qaeda in the Islamic Maghreb (AQIM), exploited the resulting political vacuum and seized control of the northern two-thirds of Mali. Terrorists enjoyed greater freedom of movement and, temporarily, access to a larger pool of potential recruits and training opportunities tapping into endless links of religious brotherhood and radicalism. At the same time, transnational criminal networks used well-established smuggling routes to develop their business opportunities. No country is immune to this phenomenon. Chad has been a steady route for illicit weapons trafficking out of Libya and towards other parts of the region where there is a high demand for weapons. The nexus between Jihadists elements and transnational organized criminal syndicates poses unprecedented challenges to a region struggling with structural crisis. The real danger is aggravated when poverty and jihad ideology come together in a volatile and chaotic region. Transnational organized crime networks are illegal businesses holdings operating throughout the world, generating massive profits without adhering to the legal principles of any government. While transnational organized crime markets and the vast profits they generate clearly continue to fuel instability and hinder development in West Africa, solid information about these markets is hard to come by[117]. There are structural elements that make organized crime successful. The main driver is poor security governance. The inadequate management and distribution of natural resources lead to corruption and in some cases perpetual armed conflicts. The Democratic Republic of Congo is a country that has vast reserves of precious minerals but where violent conflicts have been prevalent. Transnational organized crime businesses thrive, cooperating with local rebel groups to illegally acquire gold, diamonds, coltan, uranium and timber. Illegal timber logging and wildlife trafficking are common in Central Africa. Firearms' trafficking is a great danger, not in terms of money generated but rather regarding the

---

[117]   UNODC Report 25 February 2013

human misery that guns are able to inflict and the instability they can instil within the region. West Africa has witnessed a series of coups and has a number of active rebel movements that seek firearms. Most of the illicit weapons originate from legitimate stocks, so limiting the size of these stocks and keeping closer tabs on them might help reduce the problem. Most of the political instability and armed conflicts are fuelled by illicit trafficking in the light firearms funded by drugs and kidnapping. The perfect of this example was Mali: for the past few years security experts have been warning the international community about the link between international organized crime specialized in drugs and rebel groups.

In the case of the coups d'état in Mali in 2012 and Guinea Bissau in 2013, the lack of cash to pay their public servants, in particular the security forces, persuaded them to become dependent on Latin American drug traffickers to get a source of income. Ideally, good security governance in a risk prone society requires: the navy, efficient airspace control, cyber-security, and financial sector expertise to counter illicit movements of people, arms, drugs, and money, as well as to guard the country against the proliferation of weapons of mass destruction-related materials and technologies.

The Nexus factor

It is well established among international security analysts that there are in West Africa trends and patterns of behaviours attracting powerful international organized crime syndicates. Those are the Mexican, Russian and Italian Mafias, Japanese Yakuza, Chinese Triads, Turkish, and Kurdish gangs, Nigerians groups, Balkan and Hell's Angels/broker gangs. These are highly organized, well equipped, well financed, formidable and totally entrenched in their country of origin. The United States government commented that the leaders of these international drug organizations have built powerful financial, transportation, intelligence and communications empires that rival those of many small governments. For example it was estimated that Gilberto and Miguel Rodriques Orejuela, two drug cartels leaders, were worth 206 billion dollars (Peter Lilley, 2006:19). International drug cartels and gangs are purely business oriented. They trade in illicit drugs, human beings, oil, cigarettes, counterfeit medicine, firearms and toxic waste, all of which are known to illegally transit through the region. As Douglas Farah writes, "many transnational criminal organizations, networks, and terrorist groups are increasingly helping each other move products, money, weapons, personnel, and goods[118]".

In Nigeria, the general impact of the increase in religious radicalism has been multiplied by the expansion of the illegal oil refining industry. This illegal market affects the environment, polluting water sources and preventing agricultural development because of the constant damage inflicted on critical infrastructures when pipelines are sabotaged and of the negative ecological impact that the illegal refineries have, adding air pollution to the aforementioned side-effects. While the government's Joint Task Force has been created to fight against the illegal oil market in the Niger Delta, the Northern part of the country is experiencing acts of religious radicalism and extreme terrorism on a regular basis: mass killings by terrorist group Boko Haram are causing socioeconomic and political instability.

Having failed to build strong institutions for two decades, Guinea Bissau cannot have sustainable governance and leadership change without having some group banging on the doors of the presidency with guns. The same can be said about Mali: when governance and institutions became fragile, religious fundamentalists and rebels seized the opportunity to expand their area of influence in the country, with external support. The result of all this was a crisis that destroyed valuable human historical heritage items, such as ancient manuscripts from the Timbuktu library, that were burnt and the destruction of the Timbuktu shrines and that could have resulted in secession and the violent implementation of radical Islam in the North of the country. Before those events, Mali had known peace, coexistence and harmony: it was the Malian way of life. Trying to find out how and why those dramatic events happened is no easy task. As insecurity rose in the region, especially after the end of Gaddafi's regime that spread chaos and violence in Libya, states suffering from a lack of

---

[118]   DOUGLAS FARAH Terrorist-Criminal Pipelines and Criminalized States: Emerging Alliances

security governance and from a history of constitutional order disruptions became even more fragile. Mali suffered from three constitutional order disruptions due to military coups d'état: first in 1968, then in 1991 and 2012. The country has also experienced secessionist rebellion attempts: the first was in 1962-1964; the second rebellion in 1990-1995 and the last one, in 2012, led to a unilateral declaration of independence of Northern Mali. The effects of the basket of risks also warp incentives, encouraging short-term opportunism at the expense of long-term investments that could advance development. Society becomes obsessed by the conflict between identity groups, not with generating wealth or increasing national prestige. Meanwhile, formal governing bodies and regulations, disconnected from their surrounding environments, and not having become an integral part of the informal institutional frameworks that guide people's behaviour, command only superficial allegiance and compliance. Real life goes on outside them. State laws go unheeded because no one acknowledges them as legitimate. Across the world, the existence of militant groups, organized criminal gangs and the nexus between them is not a new phenomenon. In recent times, however, their manifestation and intricate linkages in Africa have become growing sources of concern at the national, regional and international levels. In West Africa in particular, "terrorist" footprints are increasing due to the activities of Al-Qaeda in the Islamic Maghreb (AQIM), the Movement for Unity and Jihad in West Africa (MUJAO), Ansar Dine, Boko Haram and Jama'atu Ansarul Musilimina Fi Biladis Sudan (Ansaru) in addition to other sleeper militant networks. Further complicating the security landscape is the increase in the outbreak of transnational organised crime that feed into the so-called terrorist loop in West Africa[119]. They also include crimes that take place in one country, but with consequences that significantly affect another country[120].

---

[119] Awanbor, F.E. (2009), "The Challenges of Transnational Crime to Nigeria's Diplomacy", in OA Onafowokan and OD Oche (eds.) Transnational Crime and Security in West Africa. Lagos: Foreign Service Academy; Ezirim, G. (2010), Transnational Organized Crimes and West African States: A Focus on Nigeria's External Relations, 1989-2006. Germany: Lambert Academic Publishing

[120] Dr. Freedom C. Onuoha is a Research Fellow at the Centre for Strategic Research and Studies, National Defence College, Abuja, Nigeria;

The growing audacity of the Nigerian group Boko Haram culminated in an anti-government revolt that it waged in July 2009, with escalating attacks targeting mainly security and law enforcement agents in addition to civilians, public infrastructures, community or religious leaders, places of worship, markets, and media. On August 26th 2011, the United Nations headquarters in Abuja was bombed, resulting in the deaths of 23 people[121]. AQIM allegedly received $70 million in ransom payments between 2006 and 2011, their favourite targets for kidnappings being westerners[122]. The AQIM assisted Nigerian affiliates, Jama'atu Ansarul Musilimina Fi Biladis Sudan (Ansaru) and Boko Haram, have carry out kidnappings, thus adding a complex dimension to the security problem. Boko Haram for instance kidnapped a French family of seven in Cameroon on 19 February 2013, transported them to Nigeria, and freed them on 18 April 2013 after allegedly collecting $3.15 million as ransom. AQIM and Boko Haram had equally relied on bank robbery. Boko Haram's presence explains the sharp rise in bank robberies in Nigeria in recent years. In 2011 alone, about 100 branches were attacked, and over 30 of these were attributed to Boko Haram[123]. Oil theft in Nigeria is another potential source of terrorism financing. According to security and intelligence operatives, crude oil theft represents a funding stream for individuals and criminal gangs with connections to militant groups. For instance, a Boko Haram commander escaped from police custody in January 2013 in Abuja, facilitated by an army of youths, who are believed to be responsible for the breaking of oil pipelines in the area[124]. Compounding this public health risk is the fact that the supply chain for medicines operates at a global level, and therefore, a concerted effort at the international level is required to effectively detect and combat the introduction of fraudulent medicines along this supply

---

[121]   Onuoha, F.C. (2012), "Boko Haram's Tactical Evolution," African Defence Forum, 4(4):33

[122]   Foster-Bowser, E. and Sanders, A (2012), "Security Threats in the Sahel and Beyond: AQIM, Boko Haram and al Shabaab,"

[123]   Thisday (2011), "Boko Haram, armed robbers attack 100 bank branches," 10 December, p.6.

[124]   Suleiman, T. (2012), "Boko Haram Siege Deepens," Tell, 6 February, p.50

chain[125]. Money laundering is another major challenge that is facing the region due to corruption, weak governance and systematically deficient rule of law institutions[126]. While poverty and unemployment are widespread, those in charge of the delivery of common goods in governing bodies can be sucked up into trafficking flows, contributing to instability and sustaining terrorism in the region[127]. Where appropriate, the private sector, civil society organizations and professional associations assist Member States in building capacity to disrupt and dismantle the organized criminal networks engaged in all stages of the illicit supply chain, in particular distribution and trafficking, to better utilize the experiences, technical expertise and resources of each organization and to create synergies with interested partners. While focus has been given to the health and regulatory aspect of this problem, it appears that less attention has been given to the issue from a criminal justice perspective[128]. The fraudulent medicines highlight a potential threat to regional health security.

The need to fight against fraudulent medicine[129], can only be made possible through strengthening of regional and international cooperation in the

---

[125] The 20th session of the Commission on Crime Prevention and Criminal Justice (CCPCJ) adopted resolution 20/6 on fraudulent medicines, otherwise referred to as falsified medicines due to concern about the involvement of organized crime in the trafficking in fraudulent medicines.

[126] The Law Enforcement, Organized Crime and Anti-Money-Laundering Unit of UNODC is responsible for carrying out the Global Programme against Money-Laundering, Proceeds of Crime and the Financing of Terrorism, which was established in 1997 in response to the mandate given to UNODC through the United Nations Convention against Illicit Traffic in Narcotic Drugs and Psychotropic Substances of 1988.

[127] The United Nations bodies and international organizations, such as the International Narcotics Control Board, the World Health Organization (WHO), the World Customs Organization and the International Criminal Police Organization, as well as, national regulatory agencies

[128] http://www.unodc.org/unodc/en/fraudulentmedicines/introduction.html

[129] From the 14 to 15 of February, 2013, in Vienna, UNODC hosted a high-level conference on the illicit trafficking of fraudulent medicines-a form of transnational organized crime which threatens public safety.

area of combating money-laundering[130] and the "twin devils", namely small arms proliferation and mercenary activities in Central and West Africa[131]. The piracy phenomenon should not be viewed from a parochial standpoint. Its impacts and consequences are higher than expected because all the countries in the Gulf of Guinea have been at a certain point victims of piracy attempts and successful attacks. The Gulf of Guinea acts of piracy clearly demonstrate that international crime is associated with sub-regional repercussions: their consequences have societal, socio-economic and security impacts and they need to be adequately and fully addressed by strong institutions of governance. West Africa and the Gulf of Guinea have some effective governments with effective security governance but paradoxically most states have limited means to fully control their territorial jurisdiction. A key factor in the globalization of crime is the increased tendency for organized criminal groups to follow the lead of transnational corporations and set up operations the countries those corporations operate in, strengthening the so-called global criminal alliances. At the 1994 United Nations Conference on International Organized Crime, United Nations Secretary General Mr Boutros-Ghali referred to an "empire of criminals". The expression used by the UNSG highlights the problem of criminal networks operating at the global level and also illustrates the fact these criminal syndicates forge relations at the highest political levels, giving them the opportunity to influence the policy making of a particular country. The current waves of high profile criminal activities taking place from the Sahel region to West Africa comes with the blessing of powerful syndicates from Venezuela and Colombia, working in collaboration with local criminal networks. The international organized criminal syndicates exploit the global political and economic integration that facilies the movement of goods and services at high velocity from one continent to another in the so-called "global village". Globalization has provided opportunities poor states to get rid of the burden of slow economic development, but the same opportunity is being used by organized criminal networks through pervasive means

---

[130] Conference of the Parties to the United Nations Convention against Transnational Organized Crime,1 December 2008

[131] The Executive Secretary of ECOWAS concept noted aimed at engaging international community

undermining good governance and the rule of law that are the drivers of economic development.

The globalization has accelerated regional economic integration, creating blocks of economic cooperation and sharing agreements that allow people to transit from one country to another more easily when the countries have common borders. However, when there is a weak or failed state, that can result in the creation of a safe passage for criminal groups across West Africa and the Gulf of Guinea coastal waters, contributing to the proliferation of illegal activities, among which is piracy. In a region where poverty is high and social safety nets inexistent, drugs money is used to provide funding for politics[132]. *"Piracy in the Gulf of Guinea costs regional countries an annual 2 billion USD, posing an increasing threat to the oil-rich region in West Africa. Insecurity can lead to a loss of confidence: maritime piracy has already caused reduced visits to the ports in the zone. In the case of Benin, whose economy is strongly dependent on the Cotonou port and whose port activities contribute almost 70 per cent to the GDP, or 7.5 billion dollars, the earnings have seen a drastic drop due to piracy[133]"*. Fisheries and marine products form part of essential food elements of the people of the Gulf of Guinea. Among the rural poorest, 40% of the regional population depends on fish as a crucial component of their diet. This livelihood is under constant threats because of illegal, unreported and unregulated fishing activities conducted by foreign vessels. Illegal fishing activities have an adverse impact on the world fish markets as they deplete stocks and availability. It is of paramount important to recognize that the process of the exploitation of maritime resources requires a regional strategy aimed at addressing securing and sustainable livelihoods and development in an environmentally responsible manner. According to Martin Murphy (2008:28) there are seven factors that contribute to piracy: "(1) legal and jurisdictional weakness; (2) favourable geography; (3) conflict and disorder; (4) under-funded law enforcement/inadequate

---

[132]   Anne Frintz Drugs the new alternative economy of West Africa Cocaine politics, http://mondediplo.com/2013/02/03drugs

[133]   Prof. Joseph Vincent Ntuda Ebode, piracy in the Gulf of Guinea costs regional, posing an increasing threat in the oil-rich region in West Africa, according to an expert of the Yaounde-II University in Cameroon. Maritime Security-June 27, 2013.

security; (5) permissive political environments; (6) cultural acceptability/ maritime tradition; and (7) promise of reward". The theme surrounding each of these factors is that piracy thrives when states are unwilling or unable to extirpate the threat. Pirates capitalize on the weaknesses of a state and reap financial rewards in the process. The nature of the threat has not changed; throughout its history, piracy has been committed by brigands who target unsuspecting seafarers for the purposes of financial gain (Murphy 2008, 21). Piracy incidents will continue to occur so long as these conditions remain favourable toward them[134]. Piracy will endanger civilians, can disrupt the economy, encourages corruption, and could trigger an environmental disaster if attacks occur in congested sea-lanes traversed by oil tankers. Cruise ships, ferries, and cargo freighters present opportunities for terrorists to inflict human casualties and economic harm. There is also concerns that extremists may seek to overcome operational hurdles by "subcontracting" to maritime criminals; however, there is no credible evidence that such a nexus is yet emerging. From 2000 to 2006, the incidence of piracy rose by 68% compared to the previous six years. During the same period, there was a modest yet discernible spike in high-profile terrorist attacks and plots at sea, such as the Super ferry 14 bombing. This proximity between piracy and terrorism is especially dangerous for energy markets: most of the world's oil and gas is shipped through the world's most piracy-infested waters[135]. According to Gal Luft and Anne Karin, sea waters cover approximately three-quarters of the globe and are home to 50,000 large ships that carry 80 percent of the world's traded cargo. The sea has always been an anarchic domain. Unlike land and air which enjoy good security governance, the sea is barely policed or controlled[136]. *"The acts of piracies since 2000 have increased due to the global proliferation of small arms fuelling, to the lack of surveillance of territorial waters with adequate security infrastructures for port-side security, thus making the vulnerabilities in maritime shipping-transportation even worse. Some analysts also fear that*

---

[134]   Eric Shea Nelson Maritime Terrorism and Piracy: *Global Security Studies, Winter 2012, Volume 3, Issue 1* 15

[135]   Gal Luft and Anne Korin, Terrorism Goes to Sea Foreign Affairs-November/ December 2004

[136]   *Ibid.*

terrorists may soon exploit the carefully calibrated freight trading system to trigger a global economic crisis, or use the container supply chain to transport weapons of mass destruction. While speculation about an emerging tactical nexus between piracy and terrorism is complicating the maritime threat picture, credible evidence to support this presumed convergence has yet to emerge. In today's global environment, transnational security challenges pose serious and dynamic challenges to national and international stability[137]". Piracy is now becoming a big concern in the Gulf of Guinea, one of the transit routes of international trade where major oil producing countries, such as Nigeria and Angola, are located. Energy security is of paramount importance for the economic advancement of the Gulf of Guinea countries. It has become the core subject of discussions among all international actors in order to try and protect crude oil production and transportation from disruptions. In the Gulf of Guinea, attacks off the coasts of Nigeria accounted for 22 of the region's 31 incidents and 28 of the crew kidnappings[138]. Piracy in the Gulf of Guinea accounted for nearly 30% of attacks (427 of 1,434) in African waters between 2003 and 2011, and that proportion is increasing. This trend is due to successful counter-piracy operations off the coast of Somalia that have reduced piracy east of Suez. Deficiencies in the Gulf of Guinea could be explained by the way maritime patrolling is conducted, and by the resources that the countries of the region have at their disposal. However, when searching for information on their maritime power capacity, a shocking tendency appears: information is rarely available to the public, and when it is, it raises questions. For example, although Togo is a small country and has only a 57 kilometers coastline, it has only two vessels that have been in service for almost 40 years[139]. Even more surprising is the maritime power of Nigeria: as of 2008, the country only had 30 ships to protect its territorial waters when its coastline is 853 kilometres long, and most of those are small vessels and it is doubtful that all of them are

---

[137] Peter Chalk, The Maritime Dimension of International Security Terrorism, Piracy, and Challenges

[138] Violence in West Africa 15 July 2013, London Somali piracy has fallen to its lowest levels since 2006, International Chamber Commerce (ICC) International Maritime Bureau (IMB).

[139] Forces Armées Togolaises http://forcesarmees.tg/index.php?option=com_conten t&task=view&id=22&Itemid=41

even operational[140]. This shows why pirate attacks and oil bunkering are on the rise: even the most powerful country in the region does not have the means to fight against problems that end up affecting the whole area, from Mauritania to Gabon. Nigeria has been blessed with large reserves of Bonny Light crude oil, a high quality type of petroleum. By the mid-1970s, Nigeria had joined the OPEC (Organization of Petroleum Exporting Countries), and the government's budget bulged with petrodollars. Even though the country has larger oil reserves than the United States and Mexico combined and that oil accounts for 95% of the country's exports and 80% of its revenue, nothing good came out of this blessing as the expected rise in the quality of life and development remains a dream. Moreover, while before the expansion of its oil industry, the country's exports consisted only of agricultural products, nowadays Nigeria has to import most of the food products it consumes. O'Neill adds that "Its annual per capita income of $1,400 is less than that of Senegal, which exports mainly fish and nuts[141]".

The proliferation of small arms and light weapons in the Sahel region poses threats to peace and security, and there are a number of illegal markets where you can get access to weapons and ammunition. Central, East and West Africa are regions with an on-going history of violent conflicts that have targeted civilians and infrastructures rather than combatants[142]. The increase in insecurity in these post-conflicts societies comes from the misuse of small arms that are abundantly available. The consequence is that small arms proliferation has been particularly devastating in Sub-Saharan Africa, where machine guns, rifles, grenades, pistols and other small arms have killed and displaced many civilians across the continent. These weapons have been used in deadly quarrels in Angola, Democratic Republic of Congo, Sudan, Uganda, Sierra Leone and Rwanda, Somalia and other African countries. The problem with post-conflict societies is

---

[140] Library of Congress (2008), *Country Studies: Nigeria*, http://memory.loc.gov/frd/cs/profiles/Nigeria.pdf

[141] O'Neill T. (2007), *Curse of the Black Gold: Hope and betrayal on the Niger Delta*, National Geographic

[142] Zebulon Takwa Small Arms Proliferation Poses Challenges in West Africa

that their problems spill over and affect the neighbouring countries shortly after the war ends. Light arms move from one country to another: in other words they are repeatedly recycled from country to country, as we have seen lately after the end of the Libyan conflict.

Central America's biggest problem is also violence and 77 per cent of all murders in the region are committed with firearms. Organized crime has access to military arms left over from the civil wars, and there have been some dramatic acts of violence. The presence of light fire arms is used to justify use of the military in policing. The Mexican organized crime groups have acquired grenades and landmines from Central American countries, in particular El Salvador, Guatemala, Honduras and Nicaragua. According to open source information, these arms were stolen from military deposits in Central America to be then sold on black markets by Mexican organized crime groups. The alleged number of illegal firearms in Central America varies from one source to another. The Oscar Arias Foundation for Peace and Human Progress in Costa Rica estimates that there are some 2.85 million illegal firearms in Central America. A recent UNODC meeting of experts in Mexico City put the figure at 3 million. There are just under 13 million men aged 15 to 64 in the seven countries of Central America. Given the overall surplus of weapons in the region, there are two sets of flows: movements of weapons within countries and across the borders within the region, and movements of weapons from Central America to other countries, particularly Colombia and Mexico. Military and police stockpiles in Honduras, El Salvador, and Guatemala have been identified as the largest sources of illegal firearms[143]. "Small arms are relatively low-tech tools of war, and due to state-driven demand, there are well over 600 suppliers around the world. With more than 550 million of them in circulation, whether newly produced, liquidated by downsizing militaries or circulated from conflict to conflict, small arms are inexpensive and easily diffused. The increasing availability of rapid-fire military assault rifles, automatic pistols and submachine guns and their distribution to non-state actors have given such actors a firepower that often exceeds that of

---

[143] Firearms within Central America Central America's biggest problem is violence, and 77% of all murders in the region are committed with a firearm, then stopping the flow of weapons to criminals should be a top priority.

police or military forces. The adoption of newly available technology into shoulder-fired rockets, mortars and light antitank weapons has magnified the presence of warring factions in civil conflicts. Small arms are easy to maintain, require little support and may last several decades. They require almost no training to use effectively, greatly increasing their use in conflicts involving informal militias and children. The flow of small arms is extremely difficult to track or monitor. Small arms and light weapons can be carried by a single soldier or light vehicle, are easily shipped or smuggled to areas of conflict and can be effectively cached in legitimate cargo, warehouses or the outdoors, often in the harshest of climates. Military, police and civilian uses: Unlike major conventional weapons, small arms and light weapons cross the dividing line separating military and police forces from the civilian population. In many countries, there has been a dramatic increase in the number and size of private militias and security firms that, in many cases, are equipped with military-type weapons[144]". Readily available and easy to use, small arms and light weapons have been the primary or sole tools of violence in almost every recent conflict dealt with by the United Nations. In the hands of irregular troops operating with scant respect for international and humanitarian law, these weapons have taken a heavy toll of human lives, with women and children accounting for nearly 80 percent of the casualties. Thus, the mandate given by the General Assembly in its resolution 50/70 B to report on the phenomenon of small arms was especially timely drawing much-needed attention to what has become a priority concern in efforts to rid the world of the scourge of war and the burden of armaments. While not by themselves causing the conflicts in which they are used, the proliferation of small arms and light weapons affects the intensity and duration of violence and encourages militancy rather than a peaceful resolution of unsettled differences. Perhaps most grievously, we see a vicious circle in which insecurity leads to a higher demand for weapons, which itself breed still greater insecurity, and so on. Some of the most protracted armed conflicts in the world at present are those in which a recurring cycle of violence, an erosion of political legitimacy and a loss of economic viability deprive a State of its authority to cope with either the causes or the consequences of

---

[144]   http://www.un.org/disarmament/education/docs/SALW_Africa.pdf

an excessive accumulation, proliferation and use of small arms. Effective measures against small arms would address both ends of that spectrum. Accumulations of small arms and light weapons by themselves do not cause the conflicts but the availability of these weapons, however, contributes towards exacerbating conflicts by increasing the lethality and duration of violence entire generations of children have been affected by encouraging a violent rather than a peaceful resolution of differences, and by generating a vicious circle of a greater sense of insecurity, which in turn leads to a greater demand for, and use of, such weapons Among the worst affected victims of recent conflicts fought primarily with small arms and light weapons are the inhabitants of some of the poorest countries in the world. Particularly vulnerable are multi-ethnic societies with a history of tension among groups. Also at risk are countries emerging from long wars of national liberation and confronted with the task of reintegrating former combatants into civil society. In many instances, weapons procured at an earlier stage for purposes of national liberation have become available for the violent overthrow of new Governments by insurgent forces or terrorists, or for acts of criminality for personal gain[145]." In most cases, the fact that the negotiation and implementation of peace accords in post-conflict scenarios do not include a quantification of existing arsenals is a source of worry for neighbouring countries. This has increased the proliferation of small arms in Africa, Asia and Central America.

When they met in Lome, Togo, in September 2011, member states of the African Union concluded that, regarding the circulation of light weapons, the enhancement of international cooperation and assistance in the fight against light weapons at the national, sub-regional regional and continental levels was of paramount importance to a successful and sustainable peace and security. Light weapons illicit proliferation in the Great Lakes Region, the Horn of Africa, West Africa and bordering states, is contributing to the rise in social violence, the promotion of corruption and other criminal behaviour that constitute threats to peace, development, stability and post conflict reconstruction. Illicit proliferation, circulation and trafficking of small arms and light weapons can only be resolved through improved

---

[145] General Assembly Resolution A/52/298, Small Arm, 27 August 1997

cooperation and coordination and by reinforcing the capacity to regulate compliance[146]."

Energy security factor

The Gulf of Guinea is home six oil producing countries, namely Angola and Nigeria followed by Equatorial Guinea, Congo Brazzaville, Gabon and Cameroon. The Gulf of Guinea remains one of the most important maritime resource coasts of the Atlantic, and it is an important maritime route for commercial shipping from Europe and America to West, Central and Southern Africa. Its proximity to Europe and North America for the transportation of the low-sulphur crude oil from the region further raises its importance in the global supply of energy[147]. The region produces about 5.4 million barrels of crude oil per day. The United States gets 15% of its supplies from the Gulf of Guinea, and China and Japan depend on it for a substantial amount of their oil and gas. It also continues to supply France and other countries of Europe. Oil companies from the West and the East have made huge investments for both onshore and offshore drilling, and since the region has the fastest rate of discovery of new oil reserves in the world, it also attracts new investments for further exploration. The underlying problem is the widespread poverty and unemployment in the Niger Delta, which made crime an attractive option despite the high risks linked with oil theft and illegal refining. The West Africa's Gulf of Guinea coastlines have huge economic importance to international trading partners including Europe, United States and Asia. The United States is expected to import a quarter of its oil from the Gulf of Guinea by 2015. 70% of Africa's oil production currently comes from the Gulf of

---

[146]   African Union Strategy to Control of Illicit Proliferation, Circulation and Trafficking of Small Arms and Light Weapons by Member States Experts, held on 26-29 September 2011, Lome, Togo

[147]   The European Union launched European Naval Force Somalia-Operation ATALANTA (EU NAVFOR-ATALANTA) within the framework of the European Common Security and Defence Policy (CSDP) and in accordance to International Law. ATALANTA in December 2008, the operation successfully perform its mission and contributes to improving maritime security off the coast of Somalia.

Guinea[148]. China has been pursuing offshore oil exploration contracts in the politically unstable nation of São Tomé and Príncipe. In 2009, Chinese petroleum corporation Sinopec acquired the Swiss company Addax which gave Beijing control over four oil blocs in the São Tomé and Príncipe-Nigeria joint development zone.

The Sinopec purchase in the Gulf of Guinea made China the leading player in the São Tomé and Príncipe oil sector. Whether the islands will actually take off as a major oil producer is still unclear, though drilling is under way and commercial production is expected to begin within a few years.

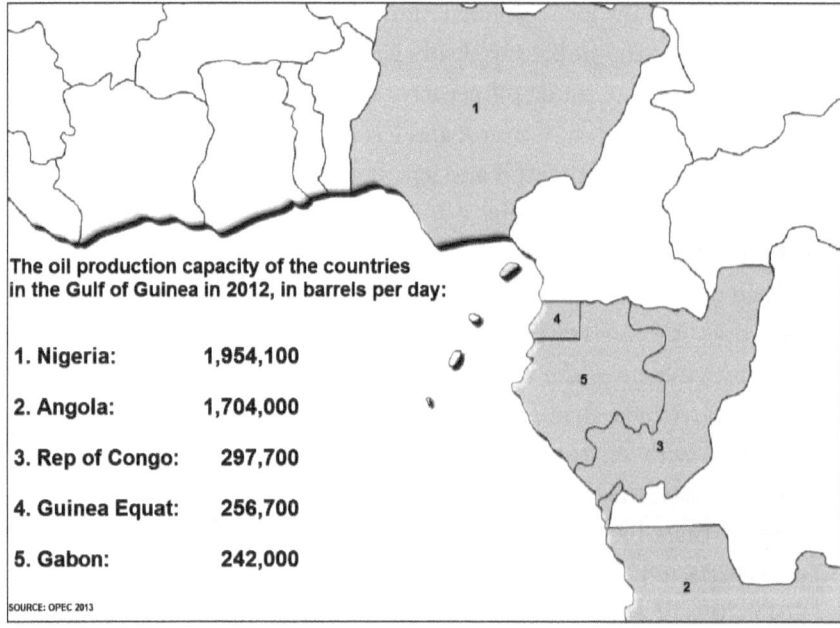

The oil production capacity of the countries in the Gulf of Guinea in 2012, in barrels per day:

1. Nigeria: 1,954,100

2. Angola: 1,704,000

3. Rep of Congo: 297,700

4. Guinea Equat: 256,700

5. Gabon: 242,000

SOURCE: OPEC 2013

In 2012, Angola's oil production grew thanks to its investments during the last decade and to its internal stability. The good governance policies that the country has adopted after the end of the civil war are allowing the country to catch up with the continent's first oil producer, Nigeria. Marred by problems such as religious extremism, piracy, poor infrastructure and corruption, production in Nigeria is decreasing. In

---

[148]   Dawit Giorgis, *why we should be watching the Gulf of Guinea.*-The Foundation for Defense of Democracies.-March 5th, 2013

2012, Angola's production reached 1,704,000 barrels per day, increasing by 5.3% compared to 2011, while Nigeria's production fell to 1,954,100 barrels per day, i.e. a 1% year-over-year decrease. The only other country in the Gulf of Guinea that had a decrease of its production from 2011 to 2012 was Gabon, but this could be considered as normal fluctuation, since it seems that its production in the last five years has also increased at times, always hovering around the 240,000 barrels per day mark. Overall, it seems that since 2008, all oil producing countries in the Gulf of Guinea have faced decreases but some of them managed to produce more in 2012, namely Angola, the Republic of Congo and Guinea Equatorial. Cameroon, which is a minor oil producing country, has produced 66,000 barrels per day in 2012, a 3.5% increase over the previous year thanks to government plans to increase production and bring it back to its old levels, when the country's production peaked at 185,000 barrels in 1986[149]. Even though regular crime is declining in Nigeria, organized crime activities keep increasing, as the rising number of kidnappings show. Recently, the no. 2 cleric of the Anglican Church in the Niger Delta region was kidnapped in Port Harcourt. While his wife was released hours after being captured, the captors held him for more than a week and he was eventually freed unharmed, even if those who had abducted him allegedly did not get money in exchange for his freedom[150]. Kidnappings-for-ransom incidents are very common in oil-rich Nigeria, although targeting religious leaders is a new strategy that the syndicates are using. Most of those kidnapped are released unharmed after ransoms have been paid, thereby contributing to the general violence in the country and tempting the other negative actors to resort to kidnappings, thus aggravating the perfect storm and strengthening the nexus between those actors. Most fundamentally, violence compromises human security and dignity—and for this reason, freedom from violence and fear is a basic human right. The 2008 Geneva Declaration on Armed Violence and Development, endorsed by more than 90 states, argues that "living free from the threat of armed violence

---

[149] Reuters February 9th 2013, *Cameroon state oil chief sees 2013 crude production up 9 pct*, http://www.reuters.com/article/2013/02/09/cameroon-crude-production-idUSL5N0B911J20130209

[150] BBC News Africa, *Archbishop Ignatius Kattey freed by Nigerian kidnappers*, http://www.bbc.co.uk/news/world-africa-24098791

is a basic human need." The political conflict that began in Liberia and spread to Sierra Leone and Côte d'Ivoire, later gave way to more organized crime across the region, as warring factions pillaged natural resources, drug trafficking networks entered the region, weakening the rule of law.

The West African security environment has deteriorated in the last decades due to traditional structural problems. The triple alliance of negative actors poses security threats that are taking on different dimensions and creating new crises that expand in the regions affected by those problems. The Sahel region is experiencing new and complex multi-dimensional threats, in particular in the Western Sahel region. Small and light arms proliferation has increased and resulted in more armed robberies, ethno-religious conflicts, assassinations, terrorism, human trafficking and kidnappings. These kinds of threats are considered to be relatively new in Sahel and West Africa. In spite of the tightened security on critical sites, several attacks have targeted western interests or companies in the Sahel desert, in Mali, Niger and Algeria. If we look further south, an oil tanker has recently been attacked off the coast of Gabon in July 2013, the first ship hijacking to happen so far south of the Gulf of Guinea[151]. According to the International Maritime Bureau there is a rise in piracy and armed robberies in the Gulf of Guinea. A few years ago, the world was caught by surprise when the Buddha statues were destroyed in Afghanistan because the Taliban said they were heretic works of art and that they needed to destroy them. This is what happens when religion and politics get hijacked by fanaticism, and it was a reaction that took by surprise the whole world, which at the time was not expecting extremism to have an impact on its historical heritage. The world was once again surprised by the speed of the growth of the political crisis in Mali and by how the same thing the Taliban had done happened again: groups affiliated to Al Qaeda attacked a local saint's tomb, destroying ancient manuscripts and shrines (US Today March 22, 2001). In the long term, those security challenges may mean higher humanitarian operating costs, higher risk and insurance premiums and a shift of resources away from the civilian labour force towards the military. The magnitude of the long-term economic consequences depends

---

[151] The Wall Street Journal, *West Africa Pirates Attack off Coast of Gabon*, July 16, 2013

on the developments of the threats perceptions and the response options taken. Chronic political instability, evident in areas marred by recurrent unconstitutional changes of government, by violent electoral processes and social conflicts, is a direct result of the lack of institutionalized political dialogue, weak parliaments and contested judicial systems.

There are three categories of refugees namely situational, persecuted and state in-exile refugees shown in the chart below, showing why they became refugees in the first place, and under what conditions they could be willing to return to their previous situation and place. Normally, when refugees leave they normally think they will able to come back home someday, after the conflict has ended, for example. However, sometimes, they can become what we decided to call here *chronic refugees*, meaning that they stay in refugee camps or outside their country for extended periods of time because the situation keeps getting worse, or stays the same. Most of the time, chronic refugees have a huge impact on the country that receives them and unfortunately represent a real burden (Michael E. Brown et al, 2004:398). Regarding the "lost generations", i.e. the refugees that were born to parents who were already refugees themselves, they tend to be more vulnerable because they have no prospect regarding their future. The lost generations represent a lost opportunity for development; instead, their loyalty is divided between the country of origin of their family and the country is which they are living. As a consequence of this, they become easy targets for terrorist groups or organized crime syndicates who are constantly looking to recruit fragile people. By the end of 2012, there were 45.2 million people forcibly displaced in the world. Of those, 15.4 million are refugees. 28.8 million of the total number are Internally Displaced People (IDP)[152]. The number of refugees of Afghan origin is due to decades of conflict that have been seriously affecting the security situation of that country and also had a big impact as a consequence on their citizens' livelihood. Successive waves of refugees have been created by the Soviet invasion of 1979-1988, then by the civil war between the Mujahedeen and the Taliban from 1989 to 1996, and lastly by the confusion that has followed the international intervention since 2001. The security situation remains unstable. This trend

---

[152] UNHCR, *New UNHCR report says global forced displacement at 18-year high.*

is likely to continue, since the coalition has started withdrawing its forces even if security has not been guaranteed and the institutions of governance are still not strong enough to maintain stability.

Ever since the creation of the State of Israel, the world has had to deal with the Palestinian refugee issues problem. The United Nations High Commissioner for Refugees estimated that there are 4.9 million Palestinian refugees. Of course, this number represents several generations of refugees. The first wave, in 1950, included of 711,000 people, i.e. "people whose normal place of residence was Palestine between June 1946 and May 1948, who lost both their homes and means of livelihood as a result of the 1948 Arab-Israeli conflict[153]." Each conflict between the Arab states and Israel has aggravated the problem, creating new waves of refugees. The last wave was created by the Intifadas. Nowadays, more than 1.4 million Palestinian refugees live in camps in Lebanon, Jordan, Syria, the Gaza Strip and the West Bank. Since the end of Saddam Hussein's regime in 2003, Iraq has lived with internal chaos. Dozens are killed on a daily basis in terrorist attacks, which makes an already unstable situation even worse. As a result, thousands have been forced to leave their hometowns to find a better place for them and their family. The United Nations High Commissioner for Refugees counts 1 million internally displaced people in the country by the end of 2013, while 746,000 have fled to other countries (534,400 in Syria and Jordan). The rest of the Iraqi refugees went to other countries in the region and to the rest of the world, but in smaller numbers. The war in Iraq has created a burden for the neighbouring countries that had to take care thousands of people fleeing violence. The case of Syria is interesting: since June 2012, 50,000 Iraqis have returned to their country of origin, while 65,000 are still there despite the civil war. The trend has now reversed, since Syrian refugees now escape towards Iraq, where there are already 160,000 of them[154]. In Colombia, decades of internal conflict have had a huge toll on the population. The government has a strong authority on the areas it controls, but in some places, its leadership is threatened and even sometimes replaced by those of rebel movements (mostly the FARC) and

---

[153] UNRWA, *Who are Palestine refugees,*

[154] UNHCR (2013), *Iraqi refugees flee war-torn Syria and seek safety back home,*

organized crime groups. At the end of 2012, there were almost 4 million IDPs, and more than 394,000 refugees in the neighbouring countries. Those are mostly situational refugees. 282,300 of those refugees are in Ecuador, Bolivia, Venezuela and Panama[155].

Since the end of Siad Barre's regime in Somalia in 1991, the country has been in continuous upheaval. There are about 1.1 million Internally Displaced Persons in the country, as well as another 1.1 million in neighbouring countries. In the neighbouring countries, there are now three generations of Somali refugees. Some of the second and third generations were born in refugee camps, while the first generation is the one that fled armed conflict and political crisis associated with a failed state. Dabaab refugee camp, in eastern Kenya, was created more than 20 years ago with an original capacity of 90,000, but, as of October 2012 had 468,000 refugees living in it[156]. About 10,000 of those refugees are from the 3rd generation, meaning that they were born in the camp to parents who were themselves born there[157].

[155] UNHCR Global Trends 2012, *Displacement: The New 21st Century Challenge*,

[156] Refugees International, *Somalia*, http://refugeesinternational.org/where-we-work/africa/somalia

[157] UNHCR, *HCR: le camp de réfugiés de Dabaab, le plus vaste du monde, a 20 ans*, http://www.un.org/apps/newsFr/storyF.asp?NewsID=27628&Cr=somaliens&Cr1#. UiB3fdIyZjR

CHAPTER IV

Who Supports the Cost of Armed Conflicts?

"Land mines are for some countries a grave obstacle, which cause both accidents and underutilization of existing productive capacity, especially in agriculture[158] "

As war-related instability affects all sectors and dimensions of societies, internal displacement or forced migration is often the only solution left for thousands, if not millions. Refugee camps are created to accommodate them while they wait to find a better way to live or while they wait for an opportunity to go back to their country or region of origin. In order to maintain stability and security in refugee camps, natural resources become even more important assets. However, while armed conflicts obviously require immense quantities of those natural resources, the return to peace does not mean that need diminishes: reconstruction of infrastructures and the resettlement of refugees or IDPs require a lot of resources as well as adding an extra strain on an already fragile equilibrium. Natural resources can be a cause for conflict, depending on the characteristics of the society that has them.

Countries that have natural resources in abundant quantities are sometimes plagued with massive economic inequalities which lead to ethnic, regional and class struggles based on the fact that some parts of the population feel left out from the country's development. The lack of equity gives way to rival nationalisms. The direct costs are sometimes hard to measure and it is often difficult to find related data but when available, they are easy to understand.

---

[158]   *Studies in conflict economics and economic growth*, Department of Peace and Conflict Research Uppsala University

The indirect costs are much more controversial since they cannot be directly seen and therefore are estimations. These can always be questioned and are sometimes built on controversial assumptions. Political deliberations are perhaps more easily influenced by budgetary items, lists of destroyed property and of human casualties. Nevertheless the indirect impacts are quite large and are of crucial importance to estimate future production capacity and thereby the potential future wealth of a country. The costs of armed conflict are heavy in terms of both economic and human dimension. Regarding the economic dimension, the following effects can occur; slowed growth, often leading to recession and a big decrease of exports, and as a result of this, the government has trouble getting foreign currency. Governments have fewer resources, and worsen their debts in order to function and continue the war. Foreign investors become wary and stop investing in countries affected by armed conflicts. In terms of human costs, armed conflicts: increase infant mortality and malnutrition; create a decline in terms of education and health standards; take a huge toll on a country's workforce, with a lot of able-bodied men being killed or permanently disabled (Stewart and Gerald 2001:230-32). In 2012, the government of Mali was overthrown by junior officer, before the scheduled presidential elections could take place. Already plagued with severe governance and statehood failure, Mali quickly got overwhelmed by the problems it had to face: the ever-increasing transnational organized crime, as well as the rapid conquest of new territories by Islamist forces, supported by the Tuaregs, who saw this as an opportunity to get revenge on a government that has always treated them as inferior citizens or second citizens in the land of their birth. The fall of Gadafi's regime also had an important impact on the internal situation in Mali, as lots of weapons from Libya ended up in the hands of the rebels in Mali. Years of poor management and leadership, combined with a lack of training and equipment, threatened the country's unity and stability.

With rebels advancing further south, French president Hollande decided in January 2013 to launch a military intervention, following the 2085

Security Council Resolution[159]. Even though the resolution calls for an African-led intervention, the AU took too much time to act and the other countries in the region were still not ready to take on the task of restoring peace. As a consequence of all this, France had to step in once again, and they successfully put an end to the fast progression of the rebels towards Bamako. On June 18th, 2013, a new peace agreement was signed between the interim government and two rebel groups, the National Movement for the Liberation of Azawad (MNLA) and the HCUA (High Council for the Unity of Azawad[160]. It paved the way for future elections (to be held on July 28th), and intends to achieve a disarmament of the rebel groups in exchange for their inclusion in the Malian society. It also took into account the recommendations made by the Security Council in Resolution 2100, among them the inclusion of international peacekeeping forces to stabilize the situation[161], especially in Kidal, the city that had been overtaken by the Tuaregs earlier. The other objectives of the intervention were ensuring that the country returned to some level of internal security, in order to make the organization of new presidential elections possible. Stability in Mali means that the stability of the region can be maintained. Had Mali fallen into the hands of the rebels, it is highly probable that this would have spread to other countries in the area. Regarding the reasons that led to the last disruption of governance, after two decades of democracy, it can be explained by the combination of the threats coming from the northern part of the country, and the fact that the military was less and less taken into account. Low salaries, lack of equipment: all these elements finally weakened the loyalty of the army. Corruption and weak security structures are also major factors that allowed the coup[162].

---

[159] *SECURITY COUNCIL AUTHORIZES DEPLOYMENT OF AFRICAN-LED INTERNATIONAL SUPPORT MISSION IN MALI FOR INITIAL YEAR-LONG PERIOD,*

[160] LeMonde, *Un accord de paix préliminaire a été signé entre les rebelles-touareg et l'Etat malien,*

[161] Security Council Resolution 2100, April 25th, 2013, http://www.un.org/en/peacekeeping/missions/minusma/documents/mali%20_2100_E_.pdf

[162] International Crisis Group, *Mali: Avoiding Escalation*, page 18, http://www.crisisgroup.org/~/media/Files/africa/west-africa/mali/189-mali-avoiding-escalation-english.pdf

The French intervention was a success, and the presidential election was held successfully in July and August, with Ibrahim Boubacar Keita being chosen as new president for the country. As had been the case after the 1978 intervention in Zaïre, France has started to withdraw its forces, while a plan of action has been set up by international players, such as the European Union, to rebuild, equip and train an efficient Malian army[163]. Since the first disruptions of governance in 1999, Ivory Coast has been facing some intense internal instability. Before that, it had enjoyed three decades of political stability and relative economic wealth. The succession crisis was followed by political and social instability, which eventually ended up cutting the country in two parts, in 2002, when rebels seized control of the North of the country. The French decided to send their troops to stabilize the country and reaffirm president Gbagbo's authority. Soldiers were sent there gradually, and eventually, 4,000 French soldiers were posted in the country to make sure the cease-fire agreements were respected, after the government and the rebels had agreed to stop fighting. This first intervention in the Ivory Coast was legitimized through a series of multilateral agreements, such as the ones with the Economic Community of West African States (ECOWAS), for example[164]. However in 2011, Gbagbo refused to accept his defeat in the elections. His refusal was reinforced by the fact that neither the African Union (AU) nor the ECOWAS did anything to facilitate the transition. Russia and South Africa prevented the UN and the Security Council from asking Gbagbo to step down and stop the campaign of terror against Ouattara's supporters[165]. Gbagbo's side even asked the "real" Ivoirians to chase foreigners from the country, referring to the presence of the French and UN forces but also to the accusations made in the past against then-president-elect Ouattara. Until the beginning of the last decade, he was often accused of not being an Ivoirian citizen. The United Nations Secretary General Ban Ki-Moon authorized a military operation to arrest him and stop the violence that

---

[163] Lewis D. for Reuters, *EU mission seeks to rebuild Mali army after U.S. faltered,*

[164] Weiss P. (2005), *L'OPÉRATION LICORNE EN CÔTE D'IVOIRE BANC D'ESSAI DE LA NOUVELLE POLITIQUE FRANÇAISE DE SÉCURITÉ EN AFRIQUE,* Annuaire Français des Relations Internationales, http://www.afri-ct.org/IMG/pdf/afri2004_weiss.pdf

[165] Dufka C. (2011), *The Case for Intervention in the Ivory Coast,* Foreign Policy-

followed the election. In this operation, the French army supported the UN peacekeeping forces. They managed to arrest the presidential couple, so that they could face the accusations of alleged crimes against humanity. Even though the widespread violence has since stopped, Ivory Coast is still recovering, and the French forces are still there, more than ten years after their arrival. The second crisis and the subsequent intervention highlighted a lack of efficiency on part of the AU, but also the fact that the most influential countries can still manage to get UN approval to intervene for their own interests[166]. It also shows that no other power in the region had enough influence, in 2002 or 2011, to intervene and work towards stabilization. The basket of threats that affected the whole of West Africa made it impossible for any of them to intervene: corruption, weak institutions, governance, and transnational organized crime took its toll on Nigeria for example, a country that should be able, thanks to its potential, to act as a regional leader and promote peace. In terms of costs, peace operations represent a heavy burden for the United Nations. Post-conflict operations usually cost more than developmental packages themselves. The chart below shows the top 10 contributors to the UN Peacekeeping operations for the year 2013, and as expected, the biggest contributors are the world's most developed countries United States of America being the top of the list 28.38%, Japan 10.83%, France 7.22%, Germany 7.14%, United Kingdom 6.68%, China 6.64%, Italy 4.45%, Russian Federation 3.15%, Canada 2.98% and Spain 2.97%[167]. The global cost of armed conflicts is supported by many countries in the world that voluntarily made additional resources available to support the United Nations Peacekeeping, Peace building, Peace enforcement and institutional building efforts, on a non-reimbursable basis. However, the global economic upheavals represent another constraint on Member States' budgets, which means that the financing of those operations sometimes suffers from a lack of

---

[166] Mbeki T. (2011), *What the World Got Wrong in Côte d'Ivoire*, Foreign Policy, http://www.foreignpolicy.com/articles/2011/04/29/what_the_world_got_wrong_in_cote_d_ivoire?page=0,0

[167] United-Nations A/67/224/Add. General Assembly /1 January 2013 to 31 December 2015/General Assembly in its resolution 67/238 and Assembly in its resolution 67/239 Source:http://www.un.org/en/peacekeeping/resources/statistics/factsheet.shtml

resources and funds because of delayed contributions. The conflict in Mali started with few hundred thousand dollars-worth of military equipment but fighting the flame is costing the donor community millions in USD. Among the biggest donors, the African Union has pledged $50 million the European Union pledged $65 million and the United States pleaded $96 million, pending Congressional approval, while Japan made the biggest contribution, pledging $120 million[168]. Another example of crisis that is quite massive in terms of costs for the international community is the Democratic Republic of Congo, a country that has been suffering from violent armed conflicts since 1998. As a result of the widespread violence and of the weakness of the government, an estimated 3.5 million people died and 3.4 million were displaced internally, and hundreds of thousands fled to neighbouring countries. The Democratic Republic of Congo United Nations Peacekeeping Operation has the largest budget of any of the current fifteen peacekeeping operations around the globe. The United Nations Organization Stabilization Mission in the Democratic Republic of the Congo (MONUSCO) has an annual cost of $1.456.378.300[169]. The process of conflict escalation is complex and unpredictable. New issues and conflicting parties can emerge, internal power struggles can alter tactics and goals, and secondary conflicts and spirals can further complicate the situation (Woodhouse et al, 2011). War and violence increases the risk of uprooting parts of the population, thus heightening the threat of chronic impoverishment and permanent dependency on welfare. One of the direct consequences of conflicts is that they drive hundreds of millions into homelessness and landlessness, pushing them into chronic economic insecurity, hardship and food insecurity.

Residual risks factor

Failed states are tense, deeply conflicted, dangerous, and contested bitterly by warring factions. Occasionally, the official authorities in a failed state

---

[168]   Vaughan J. for AFP, *Donors pledge $455.5 mn for war-torn Mali*, http://www.google.com/hostednews/afp/article/ALeqM5glqswKUGFzkqz5M9ZwdBS4V-y-aw?docId=CNG.3d07b0c56c45fb259ed215390045c6c4.211&hl=en

[169]   United Nations peacekeeping operations Administrative and budgetary 1 July 2013 to 30 June 2014

face two or more insurgencies, varieties of civil unrest, different degrees of communal discontent, and a plethora of dissent directed at the state and at groups within the state. Political goods are obtained through private or ad hoc means. Security is equated with the rule of the strong. A collapsed state exhibits a vacuum of authority. It is a mere geographical expression, a black hole into which a failed polity has fallen. There is a dark energy, but the forces of entropy have overwhelmed the radiance that hitherto provided some semblance of order and other vital political goods to the inhabitants joined by language or ethnic affinities or borders. When Somalia failed in the late 1980s, it soon collapsed. Bosnia, Lebanon, and Afghanistan collapsed more than a decade ago, and Sierra Leone collapsed in the 1990s. When those collapses occurred, sub-state actors took over, as they always do when the prime polity disappears. Those warlord actors gained control over regions and sub-regions within what had been a nation-state, built up their own local security apparatuses and mechanisms, sanctioned markets and other trading arrangements and even established an attenuated form of international relations (Brainard, 2007:9-10). Armed conflicts are and of formulating appropriate responses require large resources to avert the long term dangers. Regarding residue risks, most countries analysed in this study share certain similar characteristics. The most prevalent of those characteristics is the high level of contestation of moral influence, power and authority. Power and authority contestation are some of the drivers of armed conflicts, and in instances where such contestation happen, political violence levels are high. Moreover, that kind of contestation has often led to disruptions of constitutional order. Countries that underwent chronic constitutional order disruptions have their institutions of governance shaken and weakened.

As a result of this, the security governance was in turn affected and weakened, which in turn created environments of socio-economic uncertainty and instability, with inadequate policies fuelling poverty and unemployment, two characteristics that are aggravated by the lack of social safety nets. These weak links are exploited by non-state actors such as transnational organized crime syndicates and international terrorist networks. In some cases, they affect the situation at the local level only, but sometimes, as it has been the case after the conflicts in Libya or Iraq, the risks spill over and can affect an entire sub region. The instability status quo is then reinforced by problems such as piracy, crime, kidnappings or transnational organized crime, all of which are difficult issues to resolve due to the fact that they particularly affect the weak links in terms of security and statehood governance. Hot spots countries affected by residue risks based on the security situation are: Somalia, Iraq, Afghanistan, Syria, Libya, Mali, Guinea Bissau, Central African Republic, Democratic Republic of Congo, Sudan / South Sudan and Egypt.

Crying wolf warning

On March 2001, the world was caught by surprise when the Buddha statutes at Bamiyan, Afghanistan, were being destroyed by the Taliban regime. World religious leaders from the Christian, Buddhist and Muslim faiths and the United Nations pleaded with the Taliban leadership to spare these priceless historical statutes. This universal call was rejected. The New York's Metropolitan Museum of Art proposed to purchase the Buddha statutes and remove them from Afghanistan to be transferred to New York. This request was also rejected. After the destruction of the Buddha statues of Bamiyan, the Taliban embarked on a campaign of demolishing defenceless statues across the country. The reaction of the then Secretary General of the United Nations was as follows: "They will be doing themselves a great deal of disservice and no religious leaders from the Islamic world have supported the edict. I told them you have to respect what is sacred to others". On July, 2012 the world watched speechlessly when a video showing Islamist extremist militants linked to Al-Qaida destroying an ancient shrine in Timbuktu. This episode demonstrated that religious radicalism linked to international terrorism groups such as Al-Qaida is threatening regional and global peace and security. In the West African and Sahel regions in particular, "terrorist" footprints are increasing, due to the activities of Al-Qaeda in the Islamic Maghreb (AQIM), the Movement for Unity and Jihad in West Africa (MUJAO), Ansar Dine, Boko Haram and Jama'atu Ansarul Musilimina Fi Biladis in Sudan (Ansaru). Further complicating the security landscape is the increase in the outbreak of transnational organised crime that feeds into the so-called terrorist loops in West Africa. On June 19th 2013, representatives from Algeria, Burkina Faso, Chad, Libya, Mali, Mauritania, Morocco and Niger met in Ouagadougou, Burkina Faso, to seek a way to coordinate a response to illicit trafficking, organized crime and terrorism in the Sahel region. It is clear that terrorism and transnational organized crime are some of the contributing factors driving political crises and deterioration of security governance in the Sahel region. As a consequence many people within the region are being displaced and constantly live with chronic insecurity. The nexus between terrorism and transnational organized crime in the Sahel and West Africa does exist. This warning came from Ambassador Robert Fowler who was taken hostage by terrorist elements in the Niger in 2008 and was the United Nations Secretary General Envoy to Niger when he was kidnapped. During his dramatic experiences in captivity he concluded that there are different layers to the problem including among others, the local community where the victims' presence is monitored, the national and international networks which provide accurate itineraries that make the success of the kidnapping possible and the thriving alliances of economic convenience. "International organized criminal syndicates are highly organized, well equipped, well financed, formidable and totally entrenched in their country of origin" (Peter Lilley 2006:19).

The Colombian cartels are purely business oriented in their trade in illicit drugs, human beings, oil, cigarettes, counterfeit medicine, firearms and toxic waste. Douglas Farah writes, "Many transnational criminal organizations, networks, and terrorist groups are increasingly helping each other to move products, money, weapons, personnel, and goods.[170]" Political instability hotspots in Africa and Asia and have been mapped based on reviewing past and current political instability and instructional crises to understand the level of statehood security governance. These hotspots are plagued with unresolved problems, amongst others: a lack of political will regarding how to address and resolve what triggers chaos and violence, as well as economic, societal and political crises; frequent disruptions of

---

[170] On July 1, 2010, the U.S. Attorney for the Southern District of New York unsealed an indictment that outlined the rapid expansion of operations of transnational criminal organizations and their growing, often short-term strategic alliances with terrorist groups. These little-understood transcontinental alliances pose new security threats to the United States, as well as much of Latin America, West Africa, and Europe.

constitutional order and contestations of legitimacy, power and statehood authority. As a result, these unresolved problems turn into chronic residual insecurity risks. The attacks on critical infrastructure, such as oil pipelines, and the kidnapping of international expatriates in the Sahel region indicate that some of the most important threats to national, regional and international security no longer come from a small number of powerful, hostile states but from multitudes of unknown, invisible non-state actors, such as transnational organized criminal syndicates and terrorists, who easily gain sanctuary in failed, weak and or fragile societies. The kinds of threats in the Sahel region in the Northern area, and both East and West Sahel have similar characteristics. Its actor's methods are similar and use the same tactics and strategy. On September 21st 2013, an attack by armed gunmen on a shopping mall in Nairobi killed at least 60 people and injured more than 150. The attack was carefully orchestrated by extremist militants from the Al-Shabab group, linked to Al-Qaida. Similar methods were used in Algeria January 2013. The standoff with the heavily armed militants, holding an unknown number of hostages, continued for days. All these events demonstrate how a hostile group that stayed in the shadows for a long time can successfully plan and conduct an attack in an otherwise safe country, thanks to the failed-state neighbourhood which Somalia is remains the. Most countries that have successfully emerged from the post-conflict complex humanitarian emergency assistance phase to a post-emergency recovery and developmental assistance phase had well defined policy guidelines in place. This process is a complex and challenging one to all the stakeholders. The lessons learned demonstrate that the logical framework which advocates the one size fits all theory becomes a stumbling block to resolve the post-conflict society's complex and multifaceted dilemmas, instead of a solution. The fight against terrorism, extremism, radicalism, organized crime and their alliances require a joint effort. Not only that, the continuation of political crises and the disruption of constitutional order undermines the democratization process and, as a consequence, some of these territories are by themselves unable to contain the security challenges that include: acts of piracy, terrorism, and transnational organized crime. North-Eastern parts of Nigeria have been characterized by acts of terrorism by Boko Haram that have threatened national security since the end of the Biafra War in 1960s-1970s. The Niger Delta region remains another problem area, as there are unresolved equity issues vis-à-vis oil wealth redistribution that fuels vandalism against critical oil industry infrastructure. The statehood integrity of the Democratic Republic of Congo suffers on various fronts including political instability, rebellions from the Eastern part of the country, neighbouring countries incursions and refugee exodus. Unresolved border demarcation matters between North and South Sudan are another source of conflict. Unconsolidated institutions of security governance in the Republic of South Sudan are unable to contain inter-community tensions over natural resources: the fight for access to pastoral land in order to feed livestock can degenerate into new incidents, fuelling the "cattle war".[171] Post-conflict societies often follow the logic of the framework formula with a 'top-down' strategy that is often designed far away from the actual theatre of armed conflict and political crises. This framework formula often emphasizes a "one size fits all" strategy in rebuilding destroyed institutions of governance, peacekeeping operations, institution-building and the election of national leaders.

Fragile Neighbourhoods factor

Conflicts and political crises do not happen in isolation. Residual vulnerabilities and risks are interdependent as a consequence of "fragile neighborhoods". The fragility or the weak links of one state may have adverse impacts on the others. Some areas of the world, especially in Asia and Africa, suffer from the chronic fragile neighborhood syndrome due to unresolved or simply frozen political, historical, economical and constitutional rights. Those areas are characterized by chronic instability, be it at the political, societal or security levels. Sometimes, it can be all of those combined. This does not mean, however, that all of a region is affected by that chronic instability. The presence in those regions of at least one unstable element, such as a weak or failed state for example, can

---

[171] Bonifacio Taban Kuich June 19, 2013-Six civilians were seriously injured in a cattle camp in Unity state's Mayom county over the weekend by a group of raiders allegedly from neighbouring Tonj North county of Warrap state. The raiders managed to escape with 840 cows from the cattle camp next to Wangrang village, which is 30km from Mayom town. http://www.sudantribune.com/spip.php?article47007

have disastrous effects and therefore eventually spread and contaminate its neighbors. The largest example of a region suffering from that syndrome could be one that spreads from the coasts of West Africa to the Horn of Africa. It is unfortunate that there are many fragile states on the African continent have been affected by a wide array of crises, or post-conflict residual risks: disruptions of constitutional order, rebellions, cattle rustling, terrorism, mass kidnappings, conflicts over natural resources, transnational organized crime activities, and sometimes religious conflicts often used as lame excuse. At a local and national level, those crises and issues prevent the authorities to plan long term strategies to return to stability. At the regional level, those same crises and issues sometimes spread to neighboring countries, and sometimes even create a different kind of security and stability issues in countries that are not failing or weak, so to speak. Because of those issues, it is harder for international stakeholders to help in a sustainable manner, while a firefighter strategy is often preferred: since it is too difficult to plan long term strategies that could be doomed and fail in case of a new crisis, the international stakeholders chose to act by following a firefighter strategy, i.e. by sending personnel and funds when a crisis emerges, and not beforehand in order to prevent it. While the most effective solution would be to concentrate efforts on one area before moving onto another, the fragile neighborhood syndrome's effects mean that the crises to resolve are scattered across several regions or countries, resulting in a heavier commitment when comes the time to resolve them, both in terms of manpower and financial costs. Of course, one should not exaggerate and say for instance that the issues that Guinea-Bissau is facing are having severe consequences on the situation in Somalia. Even if the fragile neighborhood syndrome does expand beyond a country's frontiers, it remains limited to certain areas. That is why we can list four different areas that are suffering from the fragile neighborhood syndrome: West Africa, Central Africa, East Africa and Asia. In the latter, two major countries with thriving economies, namely India and Pakistan, are still entangled in one of the world's most dangerous crises which continues to divide them over the Kashmir territory, as Stanley Wolpert described in an authoritative assessment[172]. In the case of West Africa, three countries

---

[172] Stanley Wolpert (2010) India and Pakistan: Continued Conflict or Cooperation? University of California Press

are notoriously famous for their sad contribution, at various degrees, to the fragile neighborhoods syndrome in the region, namely Guinea-Bissau, Ivory Coast, and Nigeria. A clarification needs to be made before we talk about those elements, since all three have been facing different problems.

- Guinea-Bissau:

At the end of the year 2010, the European Union decided to question its decision to keep sending aid to the small West African country, which amounted to tens of millions of euros at the time. The decision was motivated by concerns about governance and law implementation in Guinea Bissau, following a disruption of constitutional order that had happened in 2010, when President Joao Bernardo Viera was assassinated on April 1st. The EU demanded the end of illegal arrests and detentions, as well as clear commitment to democratic values and to the rule of law. However, in February 2011, the EU decided to suspend its aid until positive developments would appear. The total amount was 102.8 million euros for the 2008-2013 period [173]. In July 2011, the EU Council approved a scheme of mutual commitments, which says that aid funds will be given to the authorities in Bissau if some requirements are met[174]. Those requirements included: a reform of the security sector, independent investigations regarding past assassinations, improvements of the public and administrative sectors, and a renewal of the military hierarchy. This has had little effect though. There have been several disruptions of constitutional order attempts since then, one of which was successful in May 2012. About 629 soldiers were then sent to help ease the tensions and to relieve the Angolan soldiers that had been there before the disruption of constitutional order so as to help the government in strengthening their security sector. The ECOWAS intervention troops were composed of soldiers from Burkina Faso, Nigeria and Senegal. The mere fact that a regional organization had to intervene shows one of the consequences

---

[173] Development and cooperation-Europaid, http://ec.europa.eu/europeaid/where/acp/country-cooperation/guinea-bissau/guinea-bissau_en.htm

[174] Council Decision of July 18th 2011, concerning the conclusion of consultations with the Republic of Guinea-Bissau, http://eur-lex.europa.eu/LexUriServ/LexUriServ.do?uri=OJ:L:2011:203:0002:0006:EN:PDF

of the fragile neighborhood syndrome: a crisis that had a national scope only immediately turned into a regional issue! The intervention was soon followed by a withdrawal of Angolan troops, which had been accused by the military junta responsible to the disruption of conspiring against them. The withdrawal was decided so as to ease tensions[175]. The disruption of constitutional order was followed by a rise in drug trafficking: from April to July 2012, at least 20 planes landed in Guinea Bissau in what appeared to be linked to drug trafficking activities[176]. And in April of the following year, former Navy Chief of Staff, Jose Americo Bubo Na Tchuto was arrested by the US Drug Enforcement Agency because of his implications in drug trafficking. Following his arrest, this statement was made by Manhattan U.S. Attorney Preet Bharara: *"The narco-terrorism conspiracy alleged in these indictments shows the danger that can grow unchecked in faraway places where unfortunate circumstances can allow narcotics traffickers and terrorism supporters to transact unseen at great risk to the United States and its interests. The link between narcotics traffickers and terrorists, their financers and supporters, needs to be broken wherever it is found[177]."* During the same month, the country's Military Chief, Gen. Antonio Injai, was also indicted by the US authorities and accused of selling weapons to rebels in Colombia in exchange for drugs. Unlike Na Tchuto however, Injai is still free and residing in Bissau[178]. Uncertainty still prevails today, as the elections that were once to be held in November 2013 have been postponed to the first quarter of 2014, although as of mid-February a new election day has not yet been chosen.

---

[175] *Angolan troops to leave Bissau next week-official*, http://www.reuters.com/article/2012/05/31/bissau-crisis-angola-idUSL5E8GVBP220120531

[176] Adam Nossiter for the New York Times, *Leader Ousted, Nation Is Now a Drug Haven*, http://www.nytimes.com/2012/11/02/world/africa/guinea-bissau-after-coup-is-drug-trafficking-haven.html?pagewanted=all

[177] US Attorney's Office Press Releases, http://www.justice.gov/usao/nys/pressreleases/April13/GuineaBissauArrestsPR.php

[178] Adam Nossiter for the New York Times, *U.S. Indicts Guinea-Bissau's Military Chief in Drug Case*, http://www.nytimes.com/2013/04/19/world/africa/us-indicts-guinea-bissaus-military-leader-on-drug-charges.html

- Ivory Coast:

Ivory Coast is slowly rebuilding itself after 15 years of internal instability that led to military interventions[179]. Since 2011, the country has been back to a more stable situation and a Security Council resolution adopted in the summer of 2013 states that the international military forces should see their numbers decreased by June 30th 2014, pending further withdrawals in the following year. The resolution also focuses on the role that the ONUCI should continue to play in order to bring peace and to enable economic and social development in a stable manner, by focusing on the security of civilians, by supporting the government in the reconstruction of its institutions, and by monitoring arms embargo and disarmament[180]. Peace and stability have been restored thanks to cooperation and to the commitment of the French and UN forces, of the African Union and of the ECOWAS, all of which have been supportive of Ouattara's efforts to take Ivory Coast out of its internal crisis[181]. On the downside, the costs of the reconstruction are sky high. In order to restore basic social safety nets, the European Commission gave a 180 million euros grant to help with the rebuilding efforts. France also gave assistance in the form of a 350 million euros loan[182]. While all of this helped the country get out of its internal crisis and let Ouattara's government concentrate its efforts on the rebuilding of state legitimacy, it only contributed to further deepen its foreign debt.

---

[179] The French Army had to intervene twice: first in 2002, and then in 2011, both times to protect the French nationals in the country after their safety was threatened by disruption of constitutional order attempts. www.defense.gouv.fr/operations/rci/dossier/les-forces-francaises-en-cote-d-ivoire

[180] Resolution 2112 (2013), https://www.un.org/News/Press/docs/2013/sc11082.doc.htm

[181] Yeo P., UN Keeping the Peace in Ivory Coast, http://www.betterworldcampaign.org/un-peacekeeping/web-features/un-keeping-the-peace-in-ivory-1.html

[182] Cook N. (2011), *Côte d'Ivoire Post-Gbagbo*: Crisis Recovery, Congressional Research Service, Washington DC

- Nigeria:

Even though democracy seems to be well established with no disruption of constitutional order in the past fifteen years, Nigeria can also be seen as an element contributing to the fragile neighborhood syndrome. The Federal Government's authority is constantly being challenged by rebel groups in the Niger Delta, by terrorist groups in the North, and by transnational organized crime groups. All those elements combined prevent Nigeria from benefiting fully from its natural resources: in spite of having the biggest oil reserves on the continent and being the first oil producer in Africa, social and economic development in the country are very slow, and Angola is slowly catching up and could become Africa's biggest oil producer in the next few years. From a regional perspective, the security situation is impacted since the violence, kidnappings and thefts are also being conducted by Nigerians in the neighboring countries. A French family was kidnapped in February 2013 in Cameroon by Boko Haram militants before being brought back in North-Eastern Nigeria[183]. The exact same situation happened at the end of the same year to a French priest[184]. In the meantime, the weakness and lack of equipment of the Nigerian security forces paved the way for the expansion of piracy in the Gulf of Guinea.

- Sahel region and instability:

The Sahel region represents a perfect example of how the fragile neighborhoods syndrome can extend to a whole region. All the countries of the region are being affected by the negative impacts of the syndrome, even the most stable ones, such as Chad or Ethiopia. The last crisis in Mali and the one in the Central African Republic have undermined all efforts towards development and democratization in the region.

---

[183] Le Monde (25/02/2013), *La famille française enlevée au Cameroun apparaît sur une vidéo postée sur Internet*, http://www.lemonde.fr/afrique/article/2013/02/25/une-video-de-la-famille-francaise-enlevee-au-cameroun-sur-youtube_1838707_3212.html

[184] Le Monde (15/11/2013), *Un membre de Boko Haram revendique le rapt du prêtre français*, http://www.lemonde.fr/afrique/article/2013/11/15/le-groupe-islamiste-boko-haram-revendique-le-rapt-du-pretre-francais_3514713_3212.html

It provides safe havens for armed groups that can thrive thanks to the lack of security governance. Those groups challenge the legitimacy of the states, by contributing to power and authority contestations. Their influence in Mali allowed them to make a partition of the country a possibility, until the French army intervened. Sadly enough, one year after those events the same thing happened in the Central African Republic, where chaos and violence led once again to a foreign military intervention in order to try to solve the crisis and prevent a partition of the country. In this particular case, the military intervention is probably going to last longer. According to Jean-Yves Le Drian, French Minister of Defence, this is due to the fact that the levels of hate and violence in the country are higher than in Mali for instance, something that the French army was not expecting to find there and which makes it harder to get the situation back to normal[185]. The longer it takes to solve the crisis in the Central African Republic, the longer uncertainty will prevail in the Sahel and Great Lakes regions; both of which were already facing serious security problems before the last conflict started in the Central African Republic. Instability is now becoming a concern to Chad, Niger, and Cameroon who have to deal with the mass exoduses of refugees. The risk that we are facing, in this interdependent world, is the emergence of a "new Somalia": chronic instability and state failure in the Central African Republic has to be dealt with in an adequate manner in order not to repeat the errors committed in the past decades regarding the Somalia crises. Moreover, the same problems can be found in the eastern part of the Sahel region. Since the independence of South Sudan, violent clashes have been happening along the border on a regular basis. While in this case as well, the weakness of the institutions of governance and the lack of authority on both parts of the border are to blame for the violence that prevents international stakeholders to work in order to re-establish peace, another aspect has to be taken into account: the disputes over natural resources.

---

[185] Le Figaro (15/02/2014), *L'opération militaire française en Centrafrique sera plus longue que prévu (Le Drian)*, http://www.lefigaro.fr/flash-actu/2014/02/15/97001-20140215FILWWW00090-l-operation-militaire-francaise-en-centrafrique-sera-plus-longue-que-prevu-le-drian.php

Other conflicts over natural resources happen at the national or local level: in that case, one party will start a war in order to gain control over a resource that will help it fund its fight against the central authorities: a rebel organization can seize control of the exploitation of a natural resource and use the benefits to purchase better weapons and equipment. We can take the example of the Movement for the Emancipation of the Niger Delta (MEND), a rebel group that fights against the Nigerian Federal Government because it considers that the revenues from the oil industry is not shared in a fair way and does not benefit the poorest parts of the population. The "resource curse", first defined by Auty[186], explains how under certain circumstances, the economy of a wealthy country, in terms of abundance of natural resources, will grow at a slower pace than the economy of a country that has less or no natural resources but a more diversified economy. He added that these countries are systematically affected by institutional stability issues, have recently suffered from disruptions of constitutional order, or currently have an authoritarian regime: in that case, the natural resources become a poison hampering the development of poor countries, paving the way for bigger problems such as mass corruption, high inflation rates, slow growth in the sectors of the economy that are not benefiting from the exploitation of those resources, and a brain drain. This was stated again recently by Diamond and Mosbacher, "oil booms poison the prospects for development in poor countries. The surge of easy money fuels inflation, fans waste and massive corruption, distorts exchange rates, undermines the competitiveness of traditional export sectors such as agriculture, and preempts the growth of manufacturing. Moreover, as oil prices fluctuate on world markets, oil-rich countries are often hit by what takes place in their neighbourhoods. Conflict often also erupts suddenly when resources are discovered. The tragedy of South Sudan is another example easily cited by realists. When constructing a sweeping analysis the focus on oil booms is seen to be bad news for democracy, human rights and the rule of law.

---

[186]   Auty R. (1993), *Sustaining Development in Mineral Economies: The Resource Curse Thesis*, Routledge, London

In fact, not a single developing country that derives the bulk of its export earnings from oil and gas is a democracy[187]". Moreover, as Acemoglu and Robinson put it, the African countries that have a lot of natural resources are often plagued by "extractive institutions". Extractive institutions design a country's policies so as to benefit a narrow and limited group of people while leaving no more than crumbs to the people[188]. As a consequence, armed conflicts and civil wars can start over these natural resources.

Conclusion

Overall there is some good news, as well as bad news. The good news is that there are a number of post-conflict countries from the developing world that are emerging from the post-emergency humanitarian assistance to the developmental assistance phase with a successful record. This is a positive movement as developmental assistance paves the way for economic development and job security enables good statehood governance and good security governance to create a durable peace and security, two of the main factors for this positive situation. Without peace and security in statehood governance, food security and livelihood resilience are very difficult to achieve. However there are also negative trends in certain parts of the world, especially in Africa, where some regions still lag behind. The West African security environment has deteriorated in the last decades due to traditional structural problems. The current triple alliances involving organized criminal syndicates and international terrorist groups pose security threats that are taking on new dimensions with the emergence of the internationalization of crime and terrorism, combined with religious extremism in the Sahel region. The internationalization of radicalism, extremism and transnational organized crime is superseding older threats. The proliferation and use of small arms and other light weapons has increased in armed robberies, ethno-religious conflicts, militancy, assassinations, terrorism, human trafficking and the kidnapping

---

[187] Diamond L. and Mosbacher J., Petroleum to the people.—Africa's Coming Resource Curse—and How to Avoid it », *Foreign Affairs*, Vol 92 N°5, September-October 2013

[188] Acemoglu D. and Robinson J. A. (2012), *Why Nations Fail: The Origins of Power, Prosperity, and Poverty*, Crown Business

for economic gain of multinational corporate representatives who were providing technical support for the operation of critical infrastructures, such as pipelines. The proliferation of light armaments is the consequence of the spill-over effects from fragile and chaotic neighbouring states, and has combined with easy access to explosives available in the international market. The easily available transferable knowledge from international terrorist networks through the internet has empowered clandestine local laboratories of all genres and are other indicators of the winds of negative change sweeping West Africa and the Sahel region, whose actors exploit the weak links of statehood security governance. These weak links are relatively interdependent, are detrimental to the global peace and security and often affect the livelihoods of millions of people around the world.

REFERENCES

Abadie A. and Gardeazabal J., (2003), *The Economic Costs of Conflict: A Case Study of the Basque Country,* in American Economic Review 93(1): 113-132, American Economic Association, USA

Ali H., (2011), *Estimate of the Economic Cost of Armed Conflict: A Case Study from Darfur,* Al Jazeera Centre for Studies, Doha

Allen T. and Thomas A., (2000), *Poverty and Development into the 21st century,* Oxford University Press,

Art R.J., and Richardson L., (2007), *Democracy and Counterterrorism: Lessons from the past,* United States Institute of Peace, Washington

Arunatilake N., Jayasuriya S. and Kelegama S., (2001), *The Economic Cost of the War in Sri Lanka,* World Development 29 (9), Elsevier, Netherlands

Avery D., (1998), *The Promise of High-Yield Agriculture,* Forum for Applied Research and Public Policy, USA

Ayittey G.B.N., (2011), *Defeating Dictators, Fighting tyranny in Africa and around the world,* Palgrave Macmillan

Bates R.H., (2008), *When Things Fell Apart, State Failure in Late-Century Africa*—Cambridge University Press

Bender W. and Smith M., (1997), *Population, Food, and Nutrition*, Population Bulletin, vol. 51, no. 4, Population Reference Bureau, Washington DC

Benoit E., (1973), *Defense and Economic Growth in Developing Countries*, Lexington Books, Lexington, Massachusetts

Benoit E., (1978), *Growth and Defense in Developing Countries*, Economic Development and Cultural Change 26(2), The University of Chicago Press

Bilmes L. and Stiglitz J., (2006), *The Economic Costs of the Iraq War: An Appraisal Three Years after the Beginning of the Conflict*, National Bureau of Economic Research, Cambridge, Massachusetts

Bilmes L. and Stiglitz J., (2008), *The Three Trillion Dollar War: The True Cost of the Iraq Conflict*, W. W. Norton & Company, New York

Blanford D. and Viatte G., (1996/1997), *Ensuring Global Food Security*, Organization for Economic Cooperation and Development: the OECD Observer

Bodansky Y., (1998), *Kim Jong-Il Chooses Crisis over Food as the Way to Retain Power*, Defense and Foreign Affairs Strategic Policy, Virginia, USA

Bozzoli C., Brück T. and De Groot O. J., (2009), *How Many Bucks in a Bang: On Estimation of the Economic Cost of Conflict*, Deutsches Institut für Wirtschaftsforschung, Berlin

Bozzoli C., Brück T., Drautzburg T. and Sottsas S., (2008), *Economic Costs of Mass Violent Conflicts*, Deutsches Institut für Wirtschaftsforschung, Berlin

Bozzoli C., Brück T. and Sottsas S., (2010), *A Survey of the Global Economic Cost of Conflict*, in Defence and Peace Economics 21(2), Routledge, Taylor&Francis Group

Brown L., (1998), *Food Scarcity: An Environmental Wakeup Call*, The Futurist, Maryland, USA

Brown L., (1998), *Food Scarcity: An Environmental Wakeup Call*, The Futurist, Maryland, USA

Brown L. and Halweil B., (1998), *China's Water Shortage Could Shake World Food Security*, World Watch Institute, Washington DC

Brown M.E., Cote Jr O.R., Lynn-Jonnes S.M. and Miller S.E., (2004), *New Global Dangers, Changing Dimensions of International Security*, The Mit Press Cambridge, Massachusetts-London

Brown M.E., and Rosecrance R.N., (1999), *The costs of conflict: prevention and cure in the global arena*, Rowman & Littlefield Publishers, Lanham-Boulder-New York-Oxford

Cassese A., (2001), *International Law*, Oxford University Press

Chan S., (1985), *The Impact of Defense Spending on Economic Performance: A Survey of Evidence and Problems*, Orbis, 29(3), Foreign Policy Research Institute, Elsevier, Netherland

Chen S., Loayza N.V. and Reynal-Querol M., (2007), *The Aftermath of Civil War*, World Bank Economic Review, Washington DC

Cheserek G.J., Omondi P. and Odenyo V.A.O., (2012), *Nature and Causes of Cattle Rustling among some Pastoral Communities in Kenya*, Scholarlink Research Institute Journals

Chickering A.L., Coleman I., Haley A.E., Vargas-Baron E., (2006), *Strategic Foreign Assistance, Civil Society in International Security*—Hoover Institution Press

Coebergh J., Hagan J., Rymond-Richmond W. and Parker P., (2006), *Sudan: Genocide Has Killed More than the Tsunami.* Parliamentary Brief, London

Collier P., Easterly W., Ibrahim A., Kaufmann D. and many others. Edited by Berendsen B., (2008), *Democracy and Development,* KIT Publishers, Amsterdam

Collier P., (1999), *On the Economic Consequences of Civil War,* Oxford Economic Papers 51

Collier P. and Gunning W., (1995), *War, Peace, and Private Portfolios* World Development 23(2), Elsevier, Netherlands

Collier P. and Hoeffler A., (2004), *Aid, Policy, and Growth in Post-conflict Societies,* European Economic Review 48, Elsevier, Netherland

Collier P., Hoeffler A. and Pattillo C., (1999), *Flight Capital as a Portfolio Choice,* Policy Research Working Paper Series 2066, World Bank

Collier P. and Gunning J.W., (1995), *War, Peace and Private Portfolios,* World Development, 23(2), Elsevier, Netherland

Collier P., Elliot V.L., Hegre H., Hoeffler A., Reynal-Querol M. and Sambanis N., (2003), *Breaking the conflict trap: civil war and development policy,* World Bank Publications

Cosgrove W.J and Rijsberman F.R., for the World Water Council (2000), *World Water Vision: Making Water Everybody's business,* Earthscan Publications

Crook F. and Hunter Colby W., (1996), *The Future of China's Grain Market,* USDA Agricultural Information Bulletin, No. 730

Dakurah H., Davies S. and Sampath R., (2001), *Defense Spending and Economic Growth in Developing Countries: A Causality Analysis*, Journal of Policy Modeling 23(6), Elsevier, Netherland

Desai V. and Potter R.B., (2002), *The Companion to Development Studies*, Arnold, London

DiAddario S., (1997), *Estimating the economic costs of conflict: An examination of the two-gap estimation model for the case of Nicaragua*, Oxford Development Studies, 25(1)

Dorsey J. and Opeitum S., (2002), *The Net Economic Cost of the Conflict In the Acholiland Sub-Region of Uganda*, Civil Society Organisations for Peace in Northern Uganda, Kampala

Dupont A., (1998), *The Environment and Security in Pacific Asia*, Adelphi Paper 319, International Institute for Strategic Studies London

Durch W.J., (2006) *Twenty-First Century: Peace Operations*, United States Institute of Peace

Eckstein G., (2010), *Water scarcity, conflict, and security in a climate change world: challenges and opportunities for international law and policy*, Wisconsin International Law Journal, 27 (3)

Fischer D. and Brauer J., (2003), *Twenty Questions For Peace Economics: A Research Agenda*, Defence and Peace Economics 14(3), Routledge, Taylor&Francis Group

Francis D.J., (2006), *Uniting Africa, Building Regional Peace and Security Systems*, Ashgate Publishing

Guha-Khasnobis B., Acharya S.S and Davis B., (2007), *Food Insecurity, Vulnerability and Human Rights Failure*, Palgrave Macmillan

Guillaumont P., (2009), *Caught in a trap: Identifying the least developed countries,* Economica, Paris

Hagan J., Rymond-Richmond W. and Parker P., (2005*), The Criminology of*

Genocide: The Death and Rape of Darfur, Criminology 43 (3)

Held D. & MCGrew A. and Goldblatt D. & Perraton J., (1999), *Global Transformations: Politics, Economics and Culture,* Stanford University Press

Hoeffler A. and Reynal-Querol M., (2003), *Measuring the Cost of Conflict,* Oxford:

Centre for the Studies of African Economies

Hough P., (2006), *Understanding Global Security*—Routledge, Taylor&Francis Group

Kline G., (1998), *The Affluent West and the Third World,* Forum for Applied Research and Public Policy, USA

Lilley P., (2006), *Dirty Dealing: The Untold Truth about Global Money Laundering, International Crime and Terrorism,* Kogan Page, Third Edition, London

Mendes E. and Mehmet O., (2003), *Global Governance, Economy and Law, waiting for justice,* Routledge Studies in International Law

Mills G., (2010), *Why Africa is poor: and What Africans can do about it-* Penguin Global

Mickolus E. and Stohl M., (1983), *The politics of terrorism,* Second Edition, Marcel Dekker, New York

Murdoch J.C. and Sandler T., (2002), *Economic Growth, Civil Wars, and Spatial Spillovers,* Journal of Conflict Resolution 46 (1), Sage Publications, USA

Nye J.S. Jr. and Donahue J.D., (2000), *Governance in a Globalizing World; Vision of Governance for the 21st Century,* Cambridge, Massachusetts; Brookings Institution press—Washington D.C

Peters M.M. and Shapouri S.,(1997), *Income Inequality and Food Security,* in Food Security Assessment, United States Department of Agriculture, Washington DC

Postel S.L., (1998), *Water for Food Production: Will there be enough in 2025,* in Bioscience, American Institute of Biological Sciences, USA

Ramsbotham O., Woodhouse T. and Miall H., (2011), *Contemporary Conflict Resolution*—Third edition, Polity Press, Cambridge

Rice S.E., (2004), *The Social and Economic Foundations of Peace and Security: Implications for Developed Countries,* Paper for the United Nations and Global Security, United Nations Foundation, New York

Roshandel J. and Chadha S., (2006), *Jihad and International Security*— Palgrave Macmillan

Rosegrant M.W., Cai X. and Cline S.A., (2002), *World Water and Food to 2025: Dealing with Scarcity,* International Food Policy Research Institute

Rosegrant M.W. and Sombilla M.A., (1997), *Critical Issues Suggested by Trends in Food, Population, and the Environment to the Year 2020,* in American Journal of Agricultural Economics, Oxford University Press on behalf of the Agricultural & Applied Economics Association

Roth D., Boelens R. and Zwarteveen M., (2005), *Liquid Relations: contested water rights and legal complexity,* Rutgers University Press, New Brunswick, New Jersey

Sen A. (1982), *Poverty and Famines: An Essay on Entitlement and Deprivation*, Oxford University Press

Siegel D., van de Bunt H. and Zaitch D., (2003) *Global organized crime: trends and developments*, Kluwer Academic Publishers, Dortrecht (Netherland)

Smil V., (2008), *Global Catastrophes and Trends: The Next Fifty Years,* MIT Press, Cambridge, Massachusetts-London, England

Svedberg P., (2000), *Poverty and undernutrition: theory, measurement, and policy*, Oxford University Press

Thurow R. and Kilman S., (2009), *ENOUGH: Why the world's poorest starve in an age of plenty*, Public Affairs (USA)

Trueba I. and MacMillan A., (2011), *How to end Hunger in Times of Crisis*, Fast Print Publishing (UK)

Wegerich K. and Warner J., (2001), *The Politics of Water: A Survey*, Routledge, London

Wiebe K., (2001), *The Nile River: Potential for Conflict and Cooperation in the Face of Water Degradation*, Natural Resources Journal 41.3, University of New Mexico School of Law

Wright A., (2005), *Organized Crime*, Willan Publishing, Cullompton (UK)